AN ADVENTURE IN TEXTBOOKS

1924-1960

by
JAMES M. REID

R. R. BOWKER COMPANY, New York & London   1969

Published by the R. R. Bowker Company (A XEROX COMPANY)
1180 Avenue of the Americas, New York, N. Y. 10036.

Standard Book Number: 8352-0258-5
Library of Congress Catalog Card Number: 71-88795
Printed and bound in the United States of America

Acknowledgments
Sample program from *Poetry: A Closer Look* by
James M. Reid, John Ciardi and Laurence Perrine,
© 1963 by Harcourt, Brace & World, Inc. and
reprinted with their permission.
"Stopping By Woods on a Snowy Evening" from
You Come Too by Robert Frost. Copyright 1923 by
Holt, Rinehart and Winston, Inc. Copyright 1951 by
Robert Frost. Reprinted by permission of Holt, Rinehart
and Winston, Inc.

CONTENTS

PREFACE

I HAVE WRITTEN THIS BOOK FROM MEMORY, rather than from research or documents. It is therefore a memoir, not history or autobiography. According to the definition in Beckson and Ganz *A Reader's Guide to Literary Terms* (The Noonday Press, New York, 1960) a memoir is: "An account of a person's life and experience written by himself. Where the autobiography is concerned primarily with the writer, his personal experiences, and the delineation of his characters, the memoir centers more on the world in which he has lived."

Memory, I realize, can play tricks, but it also imparts a certain unity. I have made no special effort to be objective. Rather, I have sought to tell the truth about myself and my adventure in textbooks over the thirty-six years with Harcourt Brace from 1924, when I graduated from Dartmouth, to 1960 when HB stopped being a privately held, family-dominated company and went public. I have no wish to hurt anyone, but the "truth" as I write it might. Truth exists only in the nervous systems of separate human beings and each individual necessarily puts his own imprint on his "truth." I stayed on for a few years after 1960 and helped HBW grow into one of the book publishing giants, before my retirement, which has been sweetened by the many continuing friendships of my publishing years.

To place this memoir in a sensible framework I have, in each of the first eight chapters, roughed in the political and intellectual background of the time—surely an appropriate measure in a book about publishing, which by its very nature must be sensitive to ideas and trends. I have made the book personal, but only insofar as my personal life had relevancy to publishing affairs. It is hard to keep an account like this from being self-serving, but I have tried to give the bitter with the sweet, to discredit little, and above all to credit correctly.

I have checked with a number of people, to all of whom I am most grateful: my wife Emmy, who worked for HB for ten years before I snatched her from the office; Charles A. Madison, the sage historian of book publishing (now retired from the College Department of Holt, Rinehart, & Winston); two of my great authors, Louis Untermeyer and George Gaylord Simpson, who read the sections in which they are featured; my author-companions of the High School Department, who read the whole MS, Luella B. Cook, Mary Rives Bowman, Walter Loban, and Ella Thea Smith; my son Jamie who writes rather than publishes textbooks; my daughter Annie who gave me steady encouragement; my younger son Mack who gave the galleys a sensitive and critical reading and, above all to the many colleagues at HB who helped mightily to build a fine, big textbook business. Of course, I didn't accept *all* of the suggestions of these good people but they did help. I am grateful, too, for the sympathetic editing of Anne J. Richter.

It was a good adventure and I think I'd like to do it all over again.

JAMES M. REID
Cooper Hill Road
Ridgefield, Connecticut
July 27, 1969

CHAPTER ONE

END
OF COLLEGE

(1924-1928)

"WHAT ARE YOU GOING TO DO, Reid, when you graduate in June?"
Thus John M. Mecklin, my sociology professor and friend, signaled an
end and a beginning. He closed my undergraduate career at Dartmouth
and started the wheels spinning for a new career in the great wide
world. All this took place at the soda fountain of Putnam's drug store
in Hanover, New Hampshire, in March, 1924.

"I thought I might teach."

"No," said Mecklin, "you want more action than that."

And he was right. I wanted to live and work in the world of books,
ideas, education, the world of the intellect. At the same time I wanted
the excitement of business, of competition, a chance to make some
money. So I was ripe subconsciously for Mecklin's next suggestion.

"Why don't you go into book publishing? I'll give you a letter to
my New York publisher, Alfred Harcourt." Great! And I got another
letter from John W. Young, my math professor, to his publisher:
Houghton Mifflin in Boston.

I was influenced at this crossroads by an idea of John Dewey's. It
came from his *Human Nature and Conduct*, tough required reading
in one of Mecklin's sociology courses. In essence, Dewey said that *in
the long run men become what they do*. With each job or career comes
a way of life that strongly molds the person. So, thought I at the age
of twenty-two, perhaps I can determine the kind of person I'll be at

1

forty-two or sixty-two by choosing the kind of work that will make for that kind of person.

A writer? That would be wonderful. But in all honesty, a hard-headed realistic judgment indicated I just didn't have the vast talent to become a first-class writer. Teaching, Mecklin had already disposed of. Book publishing, yes. I decided I'd rather become a first-class publisher than probably a second-class writer.

Book publishing met all the criteria. I felt I could make a successful start as a salesman, though eventually I sought the editor's chair. For I had been a salesman of one thing or another since the age of eleven when I became a PJG (Post-Journal-Gent) boy, selling the *Saturday Evening Post, Ladies Home Journal,* and the *Country Gentleman* for the Curtis Publishing Company. Surely in publishing there would be action, more action than in teaching. And a chance to work with creative people and perhaps help the creative process along. I would be living—and making a living—in the world of books and ideas, my education would never stop, and at forty-two, sixty-two, eighty-two . . . I'd be a man of ideas, steeped in them. Thus, my John Dewey dream.

Having made the decision to go into book publishing, I still had the task of winding up sixteen years of education, with a bang, if possible! I felt at this time that I had pretty much reached rock bottom in my thinking about myself and my orientation to the world. In short, I was ready to articulate my philosophy of life. Here was this thing bubbling inside me as spring vacation approached and I prepared to go to Boston and New York to nail down a job in publishing.

At the beginning of spring vacation I took the night train from White River Junction (called "the Junc" by Dartmouth men) for New York. I'd had the forethought to reserve an upper berth, for the trains out of Dartmouth at the beginning of vacations were always crowded. I meandered into the smoking compartment for a last cigarette (I had learned to smoke in Newark, N.J. the previous summer) and there ran into Roger Baldwin, Director of the American Civil Liberties Union. He was returning to his New York headquarters after making a most exciting speech about civil liberties and the Ku Klux Klan in Dartmouth Hall the night before.

I introduced myself and we fell into discussion of books, ideas, and the prospects of my career. Roger was an old hand with young men, having started years earlier when he was a social worker in St. Louis. And over the many years I knew him he always had a string of bright and lively young men at hand or coming by his home, or office, or camp. It turned out that night on the New York train that Roger, in his innocence of heavy travel at spring vacation, did not have a berth; so I offered to share my upper with him. He accepted and we landed at Grand Central next morning, both of us well rested. It isn't often that one cements a friendship that lasts upwards of forty years by sharing an upper. With us it was friendship at first sight!

1924 was the spring of Dartmouth's "Undergraduate Committee on Educational Policy," first student committee in the U.S., recognized and taken seriously by President Ernest Martin Hopkins and the college administration—a sharp contrast to the campus "confrontations" of the sixties. It was originated and headed by Hal Cowley, editor of *The Dartmouth*, the college daily newspaper, who was my friend and my roommate of sophomore year. Hal was obviously headed for a college presidency himself and in due course he did become president of Hamilton College in upper New York state. My roommate of senior year, Norman F. Maclean, editor of the college humorous magazine *The Jack-o'-Lantern*, and I were on the Undergraduate Committee. Our assignment was to go to New York this spring vacation, visit Columbia and its pioneering new survey courses, and garner what wisdom we could for our report on educational policy. Expenses paid. We talked to Irwin Edman, that wonderful intellectual elf, to Mark Van Doren, the great teacher and poet, and many deans and professors and came away much impressed with Columbia's set-up, especially their great introductory survey courses in the humanities and in social science.

Then, in Boston I took the opportunity to present my letter from Professor Young to Mr. Hoyt, the head of the Educational Department at Houghton Mifflin. After a long talk, he offered me a job as a salesman covering their school territory in northern New Jersey. Houghton Mifflin seemed old and furrowed with tradition to me, set in its ways, and the ladder upwards there full of people.

In New York I found my way to 383 Madison Avenue, a converted loft building but new, where Harcourt, Brace and Company had moved in twelve months before from its original nest in a brownstone at 1 West 47th Street. In the reception room I sat eagerly waiting on a sofa which I found later came from Constitution Hall in Philadelphia. Mr. Harcourt, it happened, couldn't see me and instead sent me in with Professor Mecklin's letter to see S. Spencer Scott, head of the Educational Department. It turned out we were both Psi U's and had much in common. He liked the fact that I had worked my own way through college, even showing a small profit, and that I not only was prepared to sell but actually had some selling experience. Although I did not conceal that my longtime interest was in the editorial end, I was ready to recognize that selling had to be an important, even essential, preliminary to editorial work. sss offered me a job at $125 a month, ($500 a month for neophytes these days!), with traveling expenses, covering the New England territory for both high schools and colleges —and I accepted right on the spot. I swallowed a bit of disappointment at going into pedestrian text, rather than romantic trade publishing. Harcourt Brace seemed to me a young, up-and-coming outfit and the prospect of helping it prosper and grow appealed more than fighting my way up the well-populated ladder at well-established Houghton Mifflin. Full of exhilaration, I took the next train back to Hanover to finish up the writing of "Free-thinking Pragmatism," my philosophy and my senior paper.

I returned to the modest room on the third floor that Norm Maclean and I shared on West Wheelock Street, and gladly sat down in front of my typewriter. My paper, my philosophy, was all ready to spill out and I wrote nearly 20,000 words in twenty hours straight, stopping only once or twice for a bit of food. This act of creation still remains a great peak of experience, a high top in exhilaration. There was of course some revision and editing on subsequent days but essentially "Free-thinking Pragmatism" stands unchanged as it poured forth in that twenty-hour flash flood.

To professional philosophers my paper, of course, would not be taken as serious or important, but my friends and most of my teachers who read it accorded it respect. For me it represented an integration of personality that enabled me to go on into the maze of adult living and the business of building a career as a whole person, with a minimum of illusion about myself and my relation to the world, and few inner conflicts to burn up and waste energy.

Now what were, what are, the main postures revealed in my paper? First of all, there was a non-religious posture. Not irreligious, but *non-religious*. I simply found that the idea of God did not help to mediate between me and the big, tough issues and problems of living. God and religion in general tended to confuse me, rather than clarify or contribute toward solutions. I was not aggressive—and I trust not obnoxious—about it. Two of my good older friends were the saintly John Dallas, who became eventually Episcopal Bishop of New Hampshire, and Roy Chamberlain, the College Chaplain, with whom I enjoyed many a tough game of handball. In this thinking I was much influenced by Hans Vaihinger's *The Philosophy of As If*, a hefty tome in Harcourt Brace's International Library of Philosophy, Psychology and Scientific Method. It connected up with much of the thought of William James and John Dewey, the American pragmatists.

Vaihinger's main point was that we deal with reality, internal and external, mainly through our mental constructs, which he called "fictions." By a process of trial and error we select those fictions which "work"; and here is the connection with William James' pragmatism, which defines the truth as "that which works."

In "Free-thinking Pragmatism" there are no absolutes. All is relative. My last "absolute" had disappeared in Professor John W. Young's course in the "Logical Foundations of Algebra and Geometry," when he brilliantly showed that a straight line is not necessarily the shortest distance between two points. It all depends on the assumptions and axioms (which fictions) you use. One set of fictions makes up Euclidean geometry, in which a straight line is the shortest distance between two points. Other sets of fictions make up non-Euclidean geometries, in one of which the shortest distance between two points is a section of a circle. Both geometries fit observed "reality" and the reason for choosing Euclidean geometry is that the calculations and manipulations involved in using it are less difficult and cumbersome than those of the non-Euclidean geometries. For some purposes one of the non-Euclidean geometries might be more convenient. In short, pick the set of fictions that is most convenient, most workable. Today, I would think, one might pick the set of fictions that best fits the computer!

A view of human nature, of course, is involved in one's philosophy. My view was taken mainly from American psychology, for I had taken many psychology courses, actually just one short of a major. I was much influenced by my psychology professor, Henry T. Moore, who became president of Skidmore College in the late twenties. He and I were also great rivals at handball and though I was handball champion of the college my senior year I could rarely beat Henry T. in singles. My view of psychology consisted primarily of the stimulus-response approach of Woodworth, the social psychology of McDougall and Trotter, and a Henry T. Moore-modified version of Freud.

One of the longtime baffling issues in philosophy is freedom vs. determinism. In my paper I worked out what was for me a reasonably satisfactory solution to this old dilemma: does man have a choice, or is he merely a victim of forces outside himself? Obviously all science rests on the proposition that this is an orderly world, that a sequence of sufficient causes lies behind each effect. All this I accepted. But, I insisted, a man with his brain can be and often is one link in a sequence of effective causes and so can exert some control over results. Man may be a pawn, but he is an active pawn, sometimes even the decisive force. Having put it all in words, I saw that now was the time to turn from philosophy to applied philosophy.

The few weeks between the high intensity of my spring vacation—the Undergraduate Committee interviews at Columbia, the exciting job at Harcourt Brace, and the spilling out of "Free-thinking Pragmatism" —sped nostalgically by. Soon after graduating "cum laude," with my Phi Beta Kappa key firmly in my hot little hand, I returned for a last summer in Denver, my old home territory overlooking the Snowy Range of the main Rocky Mountains.

S. Spencer Scott had seen to it that I had some twenty of the HB textbooks to become acquainted with before reporting for work in late August:

Fueter's *World History*. Good job by an impartial Swiss. An import.
Schevill's *A History of Europe*. Great book!
Adventures in Essay Reading, edited by the freshman staff of the University of Michigan. Good job, and good seller.

Linville's *Biology of Man and Other Organisms*. Not much spark, and never in the running for the big business in the schools.

Ella Cannon Levis' *Citizenship*, a ninth grade civics book. Good workmanlike job.

Arthur Faubel's *Economics*. Well written with a good sales case.

Helen Louise Cohen's *One Act Plays by Modern Authors*. Best of its kind.

Untermeyer's *Modern American & British Poetry*. A real pioneer book.

Christopher Morley's *Modern Essays*. Good prestige books, complete for college, shorter edition for high school.

Garrigues & Nurnberg's *Sentence Sense and Verb Usage*, by two brilliant N.Y.C. high school department heads but parochial in sales possibilities.

There were others but these I studied that summer and I knew the content in them when I reported for duty. But, of course, knowing textbooks as a student knows them is a far cry from knowing them as a textbook salesman has to know his books—and his competitors' books!

This was the summer that Ted Wood and I climbed Mount Evans, one of the great peaks in the Rockies. It is 14,265 feet high, higher than better publicized Pike's Peak or harder-to-climb Long's Peak. It is the grand climax of the Snowy Range, just sixty miles now by automobile road from Denver to the top, and its snowy summit visible 95% of the time. But in the summer of 1924 there was no automobile road.

Ted and I started from Brookvale, our summer resort that we had been going to for fifteen years, just twenty miles from the summit of Mount Evans. Ted was one of my oldest and best Denver friends, a couple of years older, and now one of Denver's top lawyers. That summer we were both in prime physical condition and we hit the trail for the summit about five on a beautiful July morning. The wagon roads past the Hicks' farm and the Evans' ranch soon gave way to the blazed trail of the government's forest rangers through the heavy pine and spruce forests. Good all the way. Mount Evans is not a hard climb. No feats of mountaineering are required and we made the top at one o'clock, just seven hours after we started. There's no water so sweet and good as the icy cold water that melts out of the eternal snows above timberline. We drank in the view too—one hundred fifty miles in all directions, the air so clean and clear. We signed the book at the top, Ted for the second time as he had climbed Evans once before with his father. By three o'clock we were down just below timberline at the ranger's cabin, where we had left our food and bedrolls for the climb to the summit. For a bit we considered pushing ourselves to hike the final thirteen miles back to Brookvale and claiming a "first" for climbing Evans and returning to Brookvale the same day. We could have done it but decided against the vanity of doing it and instead had a beautiful late afternoon and evening on the mountain and a leisurely walk back the next morning.

Finally the Denver interlude had to end. I returned east by way of my roommate's summer place at Seely Lake, Montana. Good fishing, good companionship. How we sweated it out for McAdoo in his endless battle with Al Smith for the Democratic nomination that August! John W. Davis was one anti-climax, followed by another, Calvin Coolidge. Cal's emptiness has always been signalized for me by the story of his remark, made after he had spent an hour touring the fabulous tropical gardens of Senator Dupont of Delaware. As they settled on the porch the Senator said, "Well, Mr. President, what do you think of my gardens?" Said the President, "Pretty, ain't it?" And so I left the Colorado mountains, Denver, and the sheltered life of the campus, scenes of much growth and fun, gladly—ready to do battle in the world of books, ideas, and business. To Harcourt Brace, to the New England territory, to New York!

CHAPTER TWO

THE
SELLING YEARS

(1924-1928)

AFTER MY GEMÜTLICH SUMMER IN DENVER, I arrived in New York in late August, 1924. I was a bit disturbed at the outset to find Ray Everitt, Yale '24, installed as the "bright young man" in the HB Trade Department, which at that time was most of the Company.

The Trade Department received the close supervision and personal attention of both Alfred Harcourt and Donald Brace, who had founded the company in 1919. They both, especially AH, kept an eye on the Textbook Department but the Trade Department was their true love. In late summer 1924 Harcourt Brace consisted, as I remember it, of about forty to forty-five people working on the 46th Street and Vanderbilt Avenue sides of 383 Madison Avenue. Just five years old, the Company had already outgrown its first home on West 47th Street, and, confident of its future, had leased the whole fifth floor of 383 Madison. It took us until the late 1940's to swell out and occupy the whole floor.

At the top sat AH, in his forties, at the height of his powers, and a formidable man indeed. Each day he'd make his rounds, exercising his seignorial privilege of slapping the rounded bottoms of favorite and unwary secretaries. He'd come and sit at your desk and say, "What's the scandal?" and you had the feeling that you could tell him anything. He would not only listen with real interest but come back with keen, helpful comments. At this stage he had a two-way system and it was only many years later that he became almost all broadcast and very little reception. Behind the little dark mustache and the big glasses lay a pair of large and very beautiful blue eyes. And underneath the surface dynamism lay some sadness, rarely and barely visible.

AH's wife had committed suicide, and Alfred married his longtime secretary, Ellen Knowles Eayrs, and throughout his life Ellen gave Alfred an unmatched loyalty. Alfred's only son, Hastings, was at this time in school.

Ellen Harcourt, sharing with Alfred the excitement and hard work of the early years of the Company, established the Juvenile Department, which soon became a successful division of the Company. She it was who supervised Elizabeth Bevier (later Hamilton), who carried on and built a solid, important department, with many good authors and successful books for children.

In my early years with the Company I saw little of Donald C. Brace, the balding man of iron with a gentle and mild exterior. It was he who now went to England and conducted the firm's foreign relations. Don was married to a spectacular blonde, Ida, a rare and remarkable mate for such a sedate-seeming vice-president. In the office Don had the fierce loyalty of Margaret Cuff, a devoted and able henchwoman who had in her charge all the records, royalties, etc. Ida and Margaret— what a pair!

Working directly under AH was Harrison Smith, independently wealthy from Hartford insurance money, but so much a bookman that he was a natural as editor-in-chief of the Trade Department. Hal rarely appeared on the job before eleven, but then he was always out late, patrolling literary precincts with various authors and agents through the wee small hours. Hal was a nervous, concentrated man. At times I have seen him with three lighted cigarettes—one dangling from his lips, another in his hand, and the third on an ashtray in front of him. Hal, too, had a most capable secretary, Louise Bonino, bright, fresh, attractive —from Julia Richmond High School, and later an editor of juveniles in her own right. Like Margaret Cuff and Kitty McCarthy (AH's secretary), she had graduated young and come to HB upon graduation. This school was the source through the years of much fine female talent for the company, for Mike Lucey, the principal, was a classmate of Alfred's and Don's at Columbia.

At the head of trade sales was mustachioed, cigar-smoking Gus

Gehrs, who also had a nice block of the Company's stock. The star salesman was blonde, heavy-set George Amis. Just recently trade sales had lost Ed Morehouse, whom I never met. His death apparently was a big loss. There were a couple of younger salesmen but it always surprised me how few salesmen were needed to keep a good-sized trade business rolling.

Then there was Hettie Wilson, an iron-grey widow who was head of accounting and bookkeeping, who worked late every night. And Arthur Nagle, in charge of the shipping room, a robust non-com from World War One, and his assistant, Andy Bauer, a very good bowler.

And Howard Clark, head of the Manufacturing Department, under Don Brace's supervision. Like many of the key people, Howard had come over to HB from Henry Holt & Company in 1919 when AH and Don led their revolt against the nepotism of Henry Holt and his sons to start HB.[1] Howard Clark had begun at Holt as an office boy from Brooklyn and he never quite lost his boyishness or a touch of Brooklyn accent. Almost a part of the firm were the printers with whom Howard worked: princely Richmond Mayosmith, head of Plimpton Press, who from the early beginning rightly gambled that HB one day would be a giant, and genial Jimmy Quinn, the younger of the two Quinn brothers who owned and ran our other main printer, Quinn and Boden. Other allies were Isabel Ely Lord, marvelous, solid, and scholarly queen of copy-editing, and Bob Josephy, the talented free-lance book designer.

I learned from all of these people, for I have always been willing and eager to learn from anybody, and I am grateful to them.

In 1924 the Textbook Department was *small*. It had a head (S. Spencer Scott), one editor, college only (George Shiveley), four salesmen, including me, and four or five girls. Its annual sales came to about $250,000, but it had the confidence of AH and DCB and everybody believed it was going places. Among other assets, it had the brilliant and favorable national repute of the Trade Department to build on.

In the five short years since its founding, HB had built a remarkable image. It was an inestimable advantage to the infant Textbook Department. First of all, it was an image of success, compounded of Sinclair

---

[1] *The origin and early days of* HB *are delightfully told in* Some Experiences, *by Alfred Harcourt, printed privately in 1951 and now a collector's item.*

11

Lewis's *Main Street* and his other big sellers. There was John May-nard Keynes and his vastly admired *Economic Consequences of the Peace*. And Lytton Strachey leading the way to "the new biography" with *Eminent Victorians* and *Queen Victoria*, and E. M. Forster's noble novel *Passage to India*. The International Library of Psychology, Philosophy, and Scientific Method brought great intellectual respect. Carl Sandburg . . . Louis Untermeyer and his trail-blazing antholo-gies . . . Bill Seabrook . . . Walter Lippman . . . and others.

All this meant that a salesman who walked into the office of a college teacher of literature or history or other humanity and said he was from HB found a ready hearing and a favorable attitude. The quick renown of the Company had penetrated even most high school English De-partments, though not math or science—or Latin. I remember going into the Holyoke (Mass.) High School and asking to see the head of the Latin Department. The secretary sent up my card. In due course there stumped into the office a faintly elderly lady, with a gimpy leg, head of Latin, who said she didn't need anything, thank you, from the Har-court "brace" company. When Don Brace heard this, he laughed and said: "Maybe, we ought to change the name to 'the Harcourt Brace and Truss Company.' " Such misfirings and blanks were rare, however, and I credit our speedily mushrooming and distinguished Trade De-partment for all this fine repute.

The first head of the Textbook Department had been Will D. Howe, who came to the job from Indiana University, and worked as one of the three original partners. He signed up a few books, mostly college, made some promises that he didn't keep (at certain colleges, where the the English Department was always—mysteriously—cool), and after a year or so, he left the firm. One thing I learned from Will Howe, though I never met him, was in dealing with authors always to promise less than you knew you could perform. One book that came from Howe was Strunk's *Elements of Style* and it turned out to have a curi-ous career. Published in the early twenties as a textbook for freshman English, it flopped. In the 60's, however, revived and revised by that great writer of *The New Yorker*, E. B. White, and published by Mac-millan, it had a remarkable sale, this time mostly to the trade.

To replace Howe in 1920 came S. Spencer Scott, another refugee from Henry Holt. Spence started with Holt after graduating from the

University of Michigan in 1914, where he was a tackle on the football team. For Holt he had the Connecticut territory and, I judge, made a great success of it. In World War One, sss occupied what he described as one of the softer jobs, sergeant in charge of the whiskey. He didn't get overseas. After the war he rejoined Holt for a while and, I believe, wasn't pushed along fast enough, and finally was fired. But he was picked up by HB, was allowed to buy a sizable block of stock (helped by his wife Edna's money from her father's lumber business in Oregon), and to start afresh building the textbook department. Though he became the third largest owner of the business, Spence always thought of himself as an employee and that's largely what he was until AH and DCB drew apart and sss came to hold the balance of power.

Spence's only rival—and he was considered one chiefly by Spence—was George Shiveley, the editor of the College Department and without doubt the handsomest man in the firm. Tall, dark, blue-eyed, George always fluttered the dove-cote when he'd walk down the main aisle. But he was so busy raising a family with his handsome wife, Hilda, in Bronxville that he never capitalized on his assets. George had been in the thick of the action as an ambulance driver in World War One and, as I recall, won a Croix de Guerre. He had literary taste and he could write. As a matter of fact, he wrote a novel *Initiation* by working into the wee, small hours and getting along on four or five hours of sleep a night. It was published by HB and had a modest sale. But George's talent served to split his interest between trade and text so that he never was quite single-minded in his application to the college editor's job.

Spence and George shared Arline Cone, head of girls in the Text Department. Daughter of a good New York family, she had a certain dark-eyed beauty and great charm, though technically other girls were greater secretaries. She presided over four o'clock tea from the big Russian samovar until about 1929, as I remember it, when we became too busy for all that. Arline had literary taste and intelligence which helped give the Text Department a special flavor.

The text salesmen, whose ranks I swelled by 25%, were three. Dudley Meek, the first in time and in talent by a large margin, was Wisconsin '21, son of the Toledo, Ohio, school superintendent, married to a sprightly and devoted wife, Helen, and slated to set up and head the

Chicago office. Dudley was a top salesman and a keen judge of people. At this time Dudley had most of the Middle West for his territory.

Then there were Dave Dunlap, who had the near Middle West but who didn't last very long, and H. Bertelle Gerboth who had come from Harvard a year earlier and had the East except for New England as his territory. When I discovered that the "H" stood for Hiram we quickly changed reference to him from "Bert" to "Hiram," as he continued to be known through forty-three years of service to the company. Hiram turned up in Buffalo one weekend where a chorus gal he knew was playing, when Spence thought he was in Baltimore. This incident may have slowed Hiram's progress in the department but later in the twenties he became attracted to a pretty attendant at the Macmillan booth of the textbook exhibit at Columbia summer school and in due course Ruth became his wife. Hiram was a hard-working, low-pressure, and highly successful salesman.

These were the middle twenties, when Prohibition was in flower, and the economy on its dizzy way up. Luncheons were important then as now and always, but for the most part they were without liquor. A few of us would go to Peg Woffington's, just across Madison Avenue on 47th, and the talk was lively and good. We worked a half day on Saturday and then it was that we'd seek a speak-easy for a few drinks at lunch or go to the Harvard Club where Hiram was a member. Gala lunches were held on occasion, when an important author like Louis Untermeyer or Christopher Morley came in. In the twenties, school teachers, who constituted the bulk of our text authors, rarely drank, whereas today they rarely don't!

One of the great things about working for HB turned out to be, as I had hoped, an opportunity to know and work with authors and other creative people. One of the original ideas in the founding of the HB Text Department was "Modern Books for the Schools!" This meant modern poetry (Louis Untermeyer and his great anthologies), Christopher Morley's *Modern Essays for Schools*, Helen Louise Cohen's *Modern One Act Plays*. I credit AH for this policy, but sss implemented it with enthusiasm. The high school English curriculum of the time was pretty dreary, ending in most schools with Matthew Arnold, but the English teachers were ready for the freshening breeze of twentieth century writing.

A corollary of the "modern books" idea was to involve top creative people in the building of textbooks and not rely entirely on teachers for the authorship. This corollary I made my own and down through the decades ensnared as many creative writers as I could into the preparation of textbooks: the poets, William Rose Benét and Louis Unitermeyer; Wilbur Schramm, the short story writer; Donald A. Stauffer, the literary critic; Percy Marks, the novelist who was also a college teacher; J. B. Priestley, the English novelist and dramatist; Edmund Fuller, the novelist and literary critic, to name a few. Somehow, the competition, keen as it is and usually quick to copy, never did catch on to this stratagem.

In the twenties, HB had good advisors and associates: Walter Lippman for several years; Joel Spingarn, literary critic and early friend of the Negro, a millionaire, with his waxed mustachios; Lewis Mumford, great thinker and *litteraire profundo*.[1] And the HB lawyer, Melville Cane, was not only tops in copyright and other law important to book publishing, but he was also a poet of distinction. Thus, the fringe of the company was high quality, too.

In the mid-twenties Sinclair Lewis was at his peak and Carl Sandburg just beginning to blossom not only with poems but with juveniles, the first two volumes of his great work on Lincoln, and his seminal collection of folk songs, *The American Songbag*. With me it was love at first sight for "The Songbag." For years I claimed to have sung more of the "Songbag" songs than anybody except Sandburg himself. My musical friends and I made many a long night seem short with the songs that Sandburg collected.

In the fall of 1924 I entered the corps of about twelve hundred bookmen who made up the sales forces of the sixty or so companies that made up the textbook industry. We were variously known as agents, representatives, bookmen, or textbook salesmen. We liked to think of ourselves as "bookmen." Our job was to sell textbooks for use in the colleges and schools of the nation. We "helped" college teachers, school

---

[1] *I found Mumford hard to read, in fact in some of his books almost impenetrable. It was largely because he used what he called the "biblical" system of punctuation, which resulted in sentences of gigantic length, with their colons and semi-colons seemingly interminable. I once tried to talk Mumford out of this idiosyncrasy but with little success.*

15

superintendents and principals, department heads and supervisors, text-book committees, and school teachers select their books for class use. We did little if any direct order-taking; rather, ours was missionary work during the school year and the actual orders generally came in during the summer. It was low-pressure rather than high-pressure sell-ing, but nevertheless it was fiercely competitive. I had never shied away from competition and so I waded into this new business with vigor.

My first call, at sss's suggestion, was in friendly territory—to Green-wich, Connecticut, in his old territory. I took the train and then a taxi to the high school and saw Mr. Andrews, the superintendent, and Mr. Folsom, the principal. Both were friendly and gracious to a neophyte making his first call. Mr. Folsom escorted me to see various department heads and I got an order for one set (thirty-five copies) of Darrow's *Masters of Science and Invention* from Mr. Morgan, the science head, to take back to the office. First blood!

It seemed wise to make Cambridge, Massachusetts, my headquarters. From here I could easily reach a high percentage of the three hundred high schools and forty colleges that made up the New England terri-tory. For the first few weeks I used trains and trolleys (no busses then) to visit my schools, lugging a bag of books that became heavier and heavier. By mid-October it became clear that I just had to have a car and so on my first trip to Dartmouth, after graduation, to sell textbooks there I bought a Ford runabout from Nelson Lee Smith, my former economics instructor, dormitory mate of sophomore year, and friend, for $150. In long midnight bull sessions Nels had introduced me to the idea of socialism. Eventually he left academic life for government work and was for many years a distinguished member of the Interstate Com-merce Commission in Washington.

One of the key spots in my New England territory was the Boston school system, at that time still well peppered by old-line New Eng-landers but already heavily infiltrated by the Irish Catholics. There was Will Snow, the assistant superintendent in charge of textbooks, bearded and aristocratic; Mr. Downey, the principal of English High School; Maude K. Hartwell, the cultured head of the English Department at Dorchester High School; Kenneth Beal of Mechanic Arts High School, the grammarian who later became one of my authors; and that wonderful renegade Irishman, Bill Cunningham, English head at Jamaica Plain High School, one of the best schoolteacher-writers of them all who became another of my good authors. Boston was never lush textbook territory, for the budget was sparse.

It was Boston that introduced me to pressure groups in the schools. I was trying to have Untermeyer's *Modern Poetry* put on the authorized textbook list for use in the Boston schools and I had the necessary promises of orders from eight or ten of the high schools and the recommendation of the English Council, composed of the heads of English Departments. But Mr. Snow called me into his office and said he was not supporting the recommended listing of Untermeyer. "Why?" I asked in amazement. Because it included Vachel Lindsay's "The Congo," his famous poem about the Negroes, their African origins, their slavery, and place in American life. Mr. Snow said it would offend the Negroes, who were extremely well organized in Boston. But, I protested, one of my competitors has listed a book in which the word "bastard" appears three times. "Well," said Mr. Snow, "when the bastards in this community get as well organized as the Negroes, then we'll have to do something about it!"

sss and AH, I must say, did not favor revising Untermeyer to get it listed in Boston; nor did I recommend dropping "The Congo." However, I learned from this Boston experience and was careful thereafter about touchy selections in areas where the pressure groups were well organized. I didn't, for example, in later years include "The Congo" in any of the *Adventures in Literature* anthologies, which were geared for big volume sales; or *Huckleberry Finn* on account of "nigger Jim"; or *The Merchant of Venice*, which some Jews found objectionable. Over the years I tried to go as far as possible in permitting my editors and authors freedom in making their best unfettered choices of selections, but stopping short of including a selection which we knew for sure would keep the book from selling. For there is no point in publishing a "good book" if nobody uses it—this was the guiding principle for many years.

My headquarters in New England were a room on the top floor of 5 Shady Hill Square, the home of Professor Lewis, Associate Professor of Philosophy at Harvard. My roommate was Penn Haile, fellow writer, classmate, and friend from Dartmouth. He had joined me in

Cambridge to work on a master's degree, which he finally decided was not worth all the work. Independently wealthy, he was not motivated to work too hard and soon he felt the call of Europe. But he was an "easy" roommate, thoughtful, considerate, and intellectually lively. Later on, Penn wrote a couple of books and lectured a bit, finally building a modern home in Norwich, Vermont, across the river from Dartmouth where he'd spent part of each year between trips to New York and Europe. In 1968, with poet Alexander Laing, he started *Groundswell*, to expose the "betrayal" of the country by LBJ, and now continuing as a sharp-shooting political quarterly.

I had to rise early, to arrive at my first school before eight o'clock, the unholy starting time of schools in and around Boston. But they did close early in the afternoon, leaving plenty of time for writing reports and recreation. Of course there were longer forays from home base. One of the longest always was to Maine, to sell high school books in a half-dozen of Maine's cities, and to cover Maine's colleges: Bowdoin, Colby, Bates, and the University of Maine at Orono, my furthest penetration north. Orono in mid-February is indeed an experience, even for a winter-hardened Dartmouth man. Thrice have I encountered 35° below zero: once during my sophomore year at Dartmouth, at Orono, and finally in a frame hotel at Pullman, the home of Washington State University, on a manuscript trip in the thirties!

Probably my most looked-forward-to foray from Shady Hill was the three-day one to Providence, R. I. For there was always a touch of Roger Williams free-thinking in that city, and the schools somehow seemed a bit more free-wheeling than most others in New England. An interesting day at Brown University usually developed, and, best of all, two of the most remarkable of my classmates were working for the Providence *Journal*. Claude A. Jagger, after some work at Columbia School of Journalism, had become managing editor of the *Journal* and a star reporter of his was A. J. Liebling, later of *New Yorker* fame and surely one of the best writers of our times. We often would gather late afternoon at the *Journal* office, sometimes joined by Major Malice, an Englishman who seemed strayed right out of Sheridan, and then go for planked steaks to the Narragansett Hotel nearby.

I first met Joe Liebling our sophomore year. Along with a half-dozen other sophomores, variously talented, I had entered the editorial competition of *The Dartmouth*, the daily newspaper for the college and for Hanover. The most sought-after prize would be the post of editor-in-chief in senior year. We earnest heelers had been slogging earnestly away for two or three months when a late entry loomed. It was Joe Liebling, not circular as he was later described, but hefty already, and elliptical rather than circular—especially his fine head was elliptical. In a week it became clear that Liebling could write rings around all the rest of us and he could have become editor-in-chief of *The Dartmouth* by an easy margin, succeeding Wallis E. (Pete) Howe, the 1923 editor-in-chief. But he got bored with the competition and quit. Then in our junior year he was fired from college for refusing to attend compulsory chapel.

Our paths next crossed in Providence, where Joe fell in love with one of the prettiest girls I ever met—Ann Beatrice McGinn, with midnight blue-black hair and Irish blue eyes—and he married her. Jagger, too, married a Providence girl. Soon after the marriage Ann showed signs of schizophrenia and began to have to spend part of the year in sanitariums. Joe stuck loyally by her for at least fifteen years.

All three of us migrated to New York about the same time—in the late twenties. Like Liebling, Jagger was a shy man; he had a hare lip, smoothly repaired of course, but still one knew it was there. He came to New York to become financial editor of the Associated Press and eventually its Assistant General Manager. Joe came to get a job on the New York *World* and I to become editor of the High School Department at Harcourt Brace.

In the early forties I persuaded Liebling to put together his magnificent series of pieces for the *New Yorker* about the French underground in World War Two into a book which we could sell both as a college textbook and as a trade book to the general public through bookstores. He accepted a collaborator, Eugene Sheffer, Assistant Professor of French at Columbia, to do the footnotes and exercises. It went through the works swiftly, with one of the best titles in my experience —*The Republic of Silence*—and it became a modest success. Its lengthy prologue I still think is one of Liebling's best pieces of writing.

There was a remarkable scene at a final conference, just before the MS was shuffled off to the printer. Even then Joe, as a result of high thinking, grandiose eating, and other rich living, was having trouble with the gout, and for surcease rested his foot, muffled in bandages, on a small table in my office. Across the table sat Gene Sheffer, a great person and a fine teacher, but a spastic cripple, twitching in his chair. Joe observed dryly, "This collaboration looks like the Confederate Army!"

Next morning I had a telephone call from Joe, who came right over to the office. He said he wanted the division of royalties changed from two-thirds to him and one-third to Gene to a straight 50-50 split—the first and only time in my nearly forty years of publishing when one collaborator insisted on diminishing his take and increasing his partner's. But Gene needed the money and Joe could earn $2500 for a single *New Yorker* piece.

It was in the fifties that Jagger lost out in the power struggle for the top job of general manager at the AP. When his rival got the big job, Jagger found himself out. He went to Hawaii and became public relations man for the sugar industry there. Liebling and I saw him two or three times on his annual trips to New York and always had a big dinner at some expensive restaurant—carefully chosen by Joe on Jagger's expense account—and then out for a night on the town. But Jagger, a true newspaper man underneath, hated public relations and a couple of years later shocked us all by walking one morning out into the Pacific Ocean, reported on the front page of the New York *Times*.

At the time of Liebling's death in the early sixties, he was working on a critical study of Time, Inc. for Harcourt Brace. I don't know how much of it he had ready, but only he could do a proper sardonic job on *Time* and it's a shame that Liebling will never get it done now.

sss, in his wisdom, had me report in from New England to the New York office about once a month for review of my reports, catching up on correspondence, and briefing. And I'd usually spend holidays, when schools were closed, in New York. All this was good, for it enabled me to keep in touch with people, events, and decisions at main headquarters. I could also keep an eye on Ray Everitt's progress in the Trade Department. Fairly soon sss was drawing me in on some policy decisions and occasionally even sought my advice on hiring. The times in New York also enabled me to meet and learn to know some of the good HB authors, trade and text, the most exciting of whom was the poet and anthologist, Louis Untermeyer.

Louis was in rare good form those days. He drank very little but his spirits were normally so high that he didn't require the extra push of prohibition cocktails. His puns were great and one of his greatest was a *triple* pun at breakfast. After a big night in the Village, Louis was asked what kind of an evening he'd had and with his customary lightning response he said, "Oh, a highly sexcessful one!" Our high spirits led us to attempt collaboration on an under-the-counter anthology of bar-room songs and bawdy ballads. Within a few months we had accumulated nearly a hundred possible selections and were going strong. One of our advisors was George Milburn, the fine young short-story writer from Oklahoma. He said he had a printer in his home town who would print the book for us. But tragedy intervened.

It was a February Saturday that LU and I had "conferred" on our project and he suggested that I stop in at New Haven the following Monday to see his son, Dick Untermeyer, who was a sophomore at Yale. We figured he was bound to have some fresh contributions for our bawdy collection. After a day's work up the Connecticut coast I telephoned Dick and we met that Monday evening in the lobby of the Hotel Taft for dinner. The noble and generous Untermeyer nose, as Dick said, made him easy to recognize. We had a long dinner, sparking readily back and forth and, as LU and I had hoped, Dick had several fresh contributions for the anthology, which he promised to type up and send in. He and I also promised to renew the contact as I came and went through New Haven.

Wednesday morning I sat down for breakfast at my hotel in Springfield, Massachusetts. A headline in the Springfield *Republican* hit me: Poet's Son Commits Suicide at Yale. Dick Untermeyer had been found dangling from the cord of his bathrobe in his dormitory bathroom. I could not then and did not ever believe that it was suicide. There was no dark suicidal undertone in the gay young sophomore I'd had dinner with two nights before. Suicide, impossible; accidental death, maybe.

Weeks later when I was able to get to LU once again I found that he, too, put no credence in suicide. Actually there was good reason to believe that Dick's death was indeed accidental. In New York the weekend before, Dick had mentioned to LU that he had been impressed with DeQuincy's *Confessions of an Opium Eater* and was considering doing a paper on strangulation for a writing course. It was obvious to LU and me that Dick, who lived alone and had no roommate, had been experimenting with the sensations of strangulation, had gone too far, slipped over into unconsciousness, and died.

After this, neither LU nor I had the heart to continue with our anthology of bawdy ballads. I turned the accumulated MS over to George Milburn, but neither did he ever complete it. However, nearly forty years later, LU did publish *An Uninhibited Treasury of Erotic Poetry*, a remote descendent of our aborted anthology.

All this time I was learning to sell textbooks. In those early days we held no sales meetings and what formal instruction I received came from SSS. Later, as Dudley Meek's star rose, we did have sales meetings and we learned from each other. The sales force was growing. I helped hire a young man from Vanderbilt University and the state of Alabama, for what we hoped would become our "southern territory" and SSS came back from the Pacific Coast highly pleased over hiring Ranie Burkhead to "cover" the Far West. This southern young man had been on the fringe of the Fugitive group that held such literary figures as John Crowe Ransom and Robert Penn Warren. He was himself a writer of sorts and at one of our sales meetings he contributed one of the best definitions of good textbook selling: "I ask questions," said he, "and find out what my man wants in a textbook. And then show him that our book has it."

Ranie Burkhead and his wife Cora became our rambling Pacific Coast office. Everywhere that Ranie went, Cora went, too, and she did a great deal of the paper work: reports, entries in the roadbook, follow-up letters.

After a year or so my territory was made even more extensive by the addition of the junior high schools of Manhattan and Brooklyn. SSS covered the high schools of New York City and the junior highs of the Bronx. In my Ford runabout I learned the intricacies of Brooklyn and sampled the flavor of famous New York neighborhoods: the lower East Side, Harlem, Washington Heights, Coney Island. This swelling of my territory was momentous, for it led to my first big editorial project, the founding of the *Adventures in Literature* series, which eventually reached an estimated 100,000,000 secondary school pupils.

In the New York schools I found the going slow. The people were friendly enough, the textbook budget was better than Boston's, the ordering honest, and of course the schools were big. The trouble was that HB just didn't have enough product that fitted New York schools. The break came in a big Harlem junior high school, P.S. 139, where Jacob M. Ross was principal. He was also, I found out, the chairman of a committee preparing a new literature syllabus. I proposed to SSS and AH that we ask Dr. Ross to edit a series of literature anthologies for HB. We invited Dr. Ross to lunch at Longchamps and there we worked it out.

In the summer of '27, while SSS was on the Pacific Coast and the seventh and eighth grade *Adventures* anthologies were in the works, a crisis arose. We learned that Scribner was bringing out a rival series and that they would have *two* smaller and less expensive books for each grade to compete with our one book per grade. I consulted several of my friends among the principals and discovered they felt this would give Scribner a decisive edge in competing for the literature business in the seventh and eighth grades not only in the seventy or so junior high schools but in the four hundred elementary schools with seventh and eighth grades. I reported all this to AH and he authorized me to go ahead and break up our *Adventures* volumes into 7A and 7B, 8A and 8B, and so on. At the last practical moment we switched and were able to meet the Scribner competition on even terms. Then we organized a whirlwind sales campaign. Scribner relied on its one full-time New York City salesman, Kilbourne. He was good and had many friends, but we decided to outnumber him. We brought in Hiram Gerboth and others to supplement the efforts of SSS and me. When the big New York order came in after the campaign ended, it totalled over 20,000 copies of *Adventures* books, the biggest order to that time in the history of the Textbook Department, and about twice as large, we found out, as the order for Scribner books.

The initial success of the seventh and eighth grade books encouraged SSS to engage Harry Schweikert, of St. Louis, as editor-in-chief to extend the *Adventures* series through the twelfth grade. Dudley Meek had been pressing for a literature series, especially for an anthology of American literature which he knew he and his men in the Chicago office could sell in large quantities in the Middle West. Scott Foresman had brought out its *Literature and Life* series a few years before and its success augured well for that of an intelligent and lively competitor (us!). Thus was launched the *Adventures* series, which became a major enterprise and in some later years produced as much business as the whole adult Trade Department did.

I continued to sell in New England and in New York City and to headquarter in Cambridge. My second year at Shady Hill Square, the replacement for Penn Haile as my roommate was Kenneth F. Montgomery, Dartmouth '25, who was starting in Harvard Law School. Monty was a good athlete, runner-up for the college middle-weight championship one year, and despite his light weight (only 160 pounds net) a contender for center on the varsity football team. Monty had had a difficult time freeing himself intellectually from the bindings of his religious upbringing (Catholic), but he had done it and I always admired him for achieving his independence. He was "helped" through college by a rich aunt, who in his maturity many years later left him several million dollars. But in those Cambridge days, Monty had to watch his funds carefully. He became one of the outstanding trial lawyers in Chicago.

Other Dartmouth friends and classmates were in various Harvard graduate schools and the shifting groups and alliances permitted a lively and gay "after-hours" life. We played bridge, ate in the good Boston restaurants, held cocktail parties, participated in the night life of Beacon Hill (the Greenwich Village section of Boston), golfed some, and during the football season made occasional overnight junkets to Dartmouth or Cornell to see big games. The best bridge player and best golfer of us all was Ralph L. Chappell, aptly called "the Moose" for his big-boned six feet seven inches and 260 pounds. In this period I learned to play golf—from my friends rather than from a pro, which surely was the wrong way to do it. The third year in Cambridge Monty and I moved in with two other graduate school friends at rooms on Cambridge Street. The fourth year, finding the need for a little more privacy, I left the group and joined another Dartmouth classmate and friend, Jim Wheaton, my old rival in handball, who was teaching at a private school in Brookline across the Charles River. Jim had beaten me for the college championship our junior year but I took him for it senior year. In later years Jim became high in public relations for AT&T.

Though the selling was going well, I was underneath getting a bit restless, eager to have a clear chance at the editing. I had come to the conclusion that the best selling could be done *before* publication. Why not build into a textbook the features which would enable it to outsell its competitors and thus simplify the job of the salesmen?

Putting through the seventh and eight grade *Adventures* books had given me a taste of editing. I had also worked in the office vacations and summers, particularly the long summer vacation when schools were closed for two to three months. I realize now that sss was trying me out. One of my first editorial ventures was an unhappy one: Werremeyer's *Cumulative Mathematics*, a junior high school series. I took courses at Teachers College, Columbia, to fill out my math background and worked conscientiously with our pedestrian author. But the teacher of my course at Columbia, John R. Clark, was just finishing for the World Book Company his collaboration with Raleigh Schorling of Michigan on *their* junior high school series, which took the schools by storm. It was just beginning to fade, thirty-five years and many revisions later, in the sixties when HB took over the World Book Company and finally, in this way, achieved, among other things, a top mathematics list.

A far better experience was with sparky Luella B. Cook on a high school composition book which we called *Experiments in Writing*. Luella was a good writer and teacher, and her MS had been discovered in Minneapolis by Dudley Meek, always a good talent scout as well as top salesman. Her MS needed a lot of work, especially on the grammar part, but I knew what to do to it. And Luella and I soon became a good team that worked successfully together on a dozen books over the next twenty-five years.

Spence was finding it more and more difficult to spare enough time from administration and sales for editorial work, though he did a fine job on Schweikert's *Short Stories* and Essie Chamberlain's *Essays Old and New*. I was delighted early in 1928 to be invited by sss to give up most of my New England territory the following fall and in June to come into the office full time as editor of the High School Department. Actually I continued to do some high school selling until 1940.

One of the important principles of the HB Textbook Department was that editors should sell as well as edit, a principle that helped build a big and strong business. Whether it was originally SSS's or AH's idea I don't know, but I embraced it and carried it out for many years. Not only does an editor with sales know-how build selling features into his books, but the recurring selling trips keep his experience fresh. Furthermore, a record and reputation for successful selling stand an editor in good stead in his relations with the salesmen. Without sales background, an editor is apt to be overpowered by sales in the clash of views in the arena of policy and sales meetings.

I had an alternative to the editorial chair the spring of '28. One of my great Boston friends was Charles A. (Cap) Palmer, famed through the Ivy League colleges in the early twenties as the hot trombone in the Barbary Coast Orchestra. After graduation in '23, Cap could have joined one of the big bands and made big money, but wisely he decided against the tense, hectic life of the jazz musician and instead joined his father in the family sewerpipe business. By 1928 Cap had become president of the company and he offered me the job of vice-president. The intellectual content of sewer pipes being pretty low, I found little difficulty in turning Cap down. Cap since has become a most successful writer in Hollywood. For example, he wrote the script for Disney's *The Lady and the Tramp*.

That spring of 1928 I discovered and hired Newbury LeB. Morse, Yale '28, as my successor in the New England territory and helped to ready him for the task. Big challenges were waiting for me in New York. I felt I was ready for them!

CHAPTER THREE

HIGH SCHOOL EDITOR

(1928-1932)

1928 WAS A SURGE—a surge for me personally, for HB, for the whole country. I returned from Cambridge to live in New York and to work full time in the office. For several months I lived in New Rochelle with my Dartmouth friend and classmate, Albert Brown, his mother ("the Mater" we always called her), and the kid brother Stewie, who was a more or less constant source of trouble. However, I persuaded my mother to come East in the fall so we could set up an apartment— on West 23rd Street in the Chelsea district, not far from the Chelsea Hotel where Edgar Lee Masters of *Spoon River* fame lived for so many years—and, later, more roistering poets, such as Dylan Thomas.

In the office my desk was set up in the large space which contained sss, Arline Cone, and—before he left—George Shiveley. There were many changes in the office. George Shiveley had deserted the textbook business to go with Frederick Stokes & Co. as their editor of trade books—a sad loss for me although I continued to see much of the Shiveleys outside of the office, and, I think, a real loss of brains and ability for the Company. For George was not only ornamental in his handsomeness but also he was a versatile sort of "utility outfielder" in the Company. For example, if the girls in the reception room were puzzled where to send a visitor, they'd call George.

One day into the reception room came a visitor who said he was Jesus Christ and wanted to talk to an editor. So the girls put in a hurry call for George. He sensed the need for promptness and when he

27

entered the reception room saw a little bearded man pacing up and down. The man identified himself and told George that he was planning to revise and up-date the New Testament and would we be interested. George, always a sympathetic listener, said we certainly would but before any pieces of silver could be advanced, we would need to see a sample revised chapter. J.C. departed and of course never came through with the chapter. Thus, a sure-fire best seller was lost to HB and the world.

Harrison Smith, with Louise Bonino, had left his spot as trade editor-in-chief to start his own company with Jonathan Cape, the rising English publisher who sought a platform in the U.S. Hal told me about the "silence" matches that he and AH sometimes put on when they had a difference of opinion. It was a test to see which could outlast the other and force him to break the silence first. Hal moved two blocks down 47th Street and set up Cape & Smith in an old brownstone, next to a famous speakeasy. Ray Everitt was moving up in the Trade Department and we soon became opponents at squash tennis, which we played an occasional noon hour at the nearby Yale Club. It always irked Ray that he could never beat me.

1928 was HB's first million-dollar year, with the Text Department making an increased contribution, but the Trade making the big gains with such big sellers as Sinclair Lewis's *Elmer Gantry* and Strachey's *Elizabeth and Essex*. Louis Untermeyer and I always said it was a book with lots of "essex appeal." To commemorate this great year AH and DCB decided to throw a big party as Christmas approached.

Longchamps furnished a huge bowl of punch, with a white wine base, or perhaps it was champagne even in those Prohibition days. But each prominent author and guest upon arrival would empty his hip flask into the bowl, which became stronger and stranger. Christopher Morley, Louis Untermeyer, Felix Riesenberg, Matthew Josephson, and Paul deKruif all contributed. The party picked up speed. Ray and I were moved to do acrobatics on the carpet of the big open office sss and I occupied. Katie Farrell, the cashier and a fine contralto, sat on a counter and started the singing. There was dancing far after office hours. Somehow, at this party and at others like it before our office parties were abolished (sad thought!), one of the girls would get enough liquor aboard to try and sit on Mr. Brace's lap. At this million-dollar party a sexy young thing from the mail (male?) room, tried it and started the beginning of the end of our office parties.

The American economy and life in New York City were surging, too. Jimmie Walker had succeeded Judge Hylan (called "the burro of Brooklyn" by Ring Lardner) as Mayor and a gracious soft corruptness pervaded the city. We young bucks wore derbies and carried canes on the Avenue Sundays. It was a matter of pride, too, to have a number of speakeasy cards in the wallet. Many of the speakeasies actually did have a slide in the door and you had to identify yourself to get in.

Not that the Feds gave up easily. One night two couples of us were in a raid. We were having dinner at the speakeasy next door to Cape & Smith, on the third floor of another brownstone. Suddenly there was running around and some confusion. Our waiter came to our table and said there's a raid on; just sit tight. Pretty soon a couple of men in plain clothes appeared, darted glances here and there, and disappeared. The raid was over. Later we found out that the Feds had taken the manager and the hatcheck girl. Why the hatcheck girl? We never found out.

William Faulkner was one author that Hal Smith took with him to his new firm. I don't remember that any particular tears were shed at HB, which had published just one novel of Faulkner's. On Bill Faulkner's first visit to New York he had some difficulty in sleeping and often resorted to the gin bottle to get to sleep. One night he woke up about four, reached for the gin bottle, and found it empty. So he got up, dressed, and went hopefully to the "cordial shoppe" across Third Avenue from his apartment. It was of course closed. Then Faulkner hailed a passing cab and explained his problem to the driver, who took him to a nearby speakeasy. The "boss" let him in and sat him down across a green baize table from himself. Bill explained he just wanted to buy a bottle of gin and didn't want a girl. When the "boss" insisted and got a little nasty, Faulkner, the little gamecock from Mississippi, reached across the table, snatched out the man's revolver from its arm holster, threw it into the center of the table, and said now let's fight for it! Bill woke up a bit later sitting in the doorway of his apartment house. He had been hit from behind and dumped outside. Apparently the cabbie had delivered him home. Moral: don't get into fights in New York bars or speakeasies.

Al Brown and I shortly thereafter had a supporting experience. We had been to the Capitol, a huge movie house on Broadway, and had some time to kill before catching the 11:35 to New Rochelle. We stopped in for a short beer at a bar on 46th Street. There was a scuffle beside us and, as we turned, three waiters ganged up on a somewhat spindly man in a salt and pepper suit. They hit and kicked him as he went down, blood spurting. My impulse was to try to even the odds but Al was a cooler head and restrained me. Then the bartender explained that the spindly man had stuck up the place the night before and made the mistake of returning. The rough of New York was to be found, we verified, never too far under the civilized, smooth surface.

The economy—and the stock market—had been going up for years and we all assumed that they would continue to rise world without end. About this time, like most everyone else at HB, I began to dabble a bit in stocks. There was Sidney Weinberg at Goldman Sachs making a splurge on Wall Street. And Sunray Oil, which AH, SSS, and others in the office saw as a real comer. It was—eventually.

This was the time of the New York *World*, beloved of intellectuals and the literati. At its apogee, it had Heywood Broun's column, FPA's "The Conning Tower," and liberal editorials. We went much to the theatre. There was, most spectacularly, Eugene O'Neill's *Strange Interlude*, five hours long, in two sections, with time out for dinner between. Great play, great acting, sensationally new and different—it furnished the base for much talk over cocktails. Then came *Show Boat* with its wonderful tunes and a not-bad story to set the American musical show a giant step ahead. And many more. Lots of good theatre.

The Book-of-the-Month Club was on the rise and so were *The New Yorker* and *Time*. I managed to be in on some of the excitement and to get to know some of the people, through my HB and Dartmouth friends and connections. I saw something of Philip Wylie before he published his first book. We drank and Indian-wrestled together (he usually won). Phil's success as a writer was no accident. He said he wrote two million words before he had a book published. I believed him—still do, for he is as fabulous as some of his characters. I took the MS of his first book to HB where it was turned down in a week—Ray Everitt's work,

I always thought. Knopf took it and Phil was on his way to a great career. Another writer of great later success I persuaded to try HB was Dr. Seuss, whom I knew as Ted Geisel, Dartmouth '25. An early MS of his, too, was turned down at HB.

I saw a good deal of Ted and his fine wife Helen those early years, before he started his meteoric rise with his famous advertisement, "Quick, Henry, the Flit." I even was one of the animals in his fantastical zoo. I was "The Paniph," a strange bird-like but earthbound creature equipped mainly with enormously cleated football shoes on my feet and grapefruit in hand. The grapefruit was a reference to the time at Winter Carnival when Ted and I threw a grapefruit into the darkened billiard room of the Psi U house and hit a chaperone in the head. Ted succeeded my roommate of senior year as editor of the *Jack-o'-Lantern*. Throughout his long and fabulous career, Ted has never lost his fine gentle character or his capacity for friendship.

In the editorial work of the High School Department I found few established procedures or practices. In fact, I was not only the only editor but also the only editorial employee. I was tempted to try to snatch Marian Abernethy, one of Mike Lucey's bright girls from Julia Richmond High School whom I had discovered sitting, mouselike, in the row of correspondents in early 1925, but she eventually succeeded Arline Cone as SSS's secretary and head girl. Instead I hired another of Mike Lucey's girls, sixteen-year-old Rose (Arancam for her Hungarian descent) Kuchta shortly after starting the high school editorial work. She was the fastest stenographer I ever worked with and she had a genius for organizing detail—a great gift for a young editor to find, for the great masses of detail in any editorial department must permanently be in good order. Only lack in Rose was that she had difficulty in composing letters on her own. I always had to dictate them all to her.

I found that the Chicago office was prospering and growing. Dudley Meek, with his genius for sniffing out talent, had hired several travelers, among them Ted Purintun, bright, intellectual, and brittle, and Lee Deighton, a real powerhouse. Soon there began to drift in from Chicago odd, slightly hostile stories about me, originating, I found out later, with DM. This was the first sign of a power struggle, but the struggle disappeared or went underground for many years. Dudley finally satisfied himself that I was a good editor and turned off the sabotage.

Soon I was hipdeep in MSS: early volumes of the *Adventures* series, *Using English*, by Lucy Chapman of the Ethical Culture School in New York, and *Exploring American History*, by Mabel Casner, seventh and eighth grade teacher at West Haven, Connecticut, and Professor Ralph Henry Gabriel of Yale.

The earliest challenge to my editorial talents after receiving the responsibility for editing HB's high school books was to build a winner in one of the largest high school markets, ninth and tenth grade composition and grammar and we had in the office a MS by Lucy Chapman. This big market was largely occupied by Hitchcock's *Composition and Grammar*, ironically, one of Henry Holt & Company's big sellers. It would be Harcourt vs. Holt in a new competition. The other main competitor was Ward's *Sentence and Theme*, published by Scott Foresman, even then one of the biggest and most formidable of the textbook publishers (all text, no trade).

Miss Chapman turned out to be a good and interesting writer, flexible and easy to work with. Her materials had been tried out over a good many years on her own classes and carefully winnowed. What her MS mainly needed was the firmness of an obvious organization, so clear that teachers of varying approaches would feel they could gain easy access to Miss Chapman's interesting materials, and a dramatizing of her way of teaching grammar.

The Hitchcock book was a loosely organized collection of shrewd and inviting teaching materials which encouraged teachers to help themselves. In contrast, the Ward book was tightly organized, lesson by lesson, a lockstep book, as our salesmen were to say in attacking it. Ward was himself not only a great teacher but he had a great one as his editor, Lindsay Todd Damon, of Brown University, who edited Scott Foresman's English books in addition to his full-time teaching job. It was Damon who thought of putting all of one school year's reading in one handy volume, and thus started *Literature and Life*, first of the two great literature series that dominated the high school literature curriculum for over three decades.

Steady application of the seat of the pants to the seat of the editorial chair with Miss Chapman's MS on the desk in front of me was sufficient to bring the needed firmness of organization. Then I dug far back into my past for an idea to dramatize her teaching of grammar. I remembered the wonderful teaching cartoons in a booklet "How to Sell the Post, Journal, and Gent," published by the Curtis Publishing Company to teach boys how to sell their magazines. Those ingenious cartoons had stuck in my mind from studying the booklet at age twelve in Denver to age twenty-six editing textbooks in New York. I wrote Curtis for a copy, found it still in print, and the cartoons as good as I had remembered them. The artist turned out to be Fred G. Cooper (FGC), active as a free-lance in New York and as a cartoonist for *Life*, the pre-Luce *Life* that was a small-format humorous magazine.

I got in touch with FGC and brought his quick intelligence and ingenuity to help Miss Chapman and me dramatize grammar. Over a period of several months, we worked out a set of about fifty cartoons to help high school freshmen understand grammar, to increase the visual appeal of Chapman's *Using English*—and help HB salesmen to win adoptions against Holt and Scott Foresman. First of all we decided against the easy way of simple decoration or of simply trying for a laugh. We insisted that each of FGC's drawings *teach*, dramatize a point, or make something important easier to remember. We wanted to make ourselves invulnerable against the claim that the cartoons were "frills" or that we were "cheapening" or downgrading in any way the teaching of grammar. Each cartoon had to function, not decorate or merely draw snickers.

Well, it worked. Chapman's *Using English* was published in the spring of 1929 and it quickly became the HB Text Department best seller of this period. The cartoons helped to draw interested attention and within a few years cartoons became "standard equipment" in grammar and composition books. The competitors, as almost always, imitated a good thing. About 1940 cartoons became "old hat" and a liability, completing a familiar cycle. Thus *Using English* was one of my first successes. In the early thirties we persuaded Luella B. Cook to revise her *Experiments in Writing* in the *Using English* format and it became *Using English: Book Two* for the eleventh and twelfth grades. And so the salesmen had a series, always a strong sales position. The *Using English* series did well in the thirties, achieved a Texas adoption in 1935 (a big thing!), was broken up into four books, one for each grade, nine through twelve, and generally prospered until Heath's series by Tressler came along and captured the bulk of the grammar and composition market and held it, despite our best efforts, until the early sixties when our Warriner series broke the Tressler stranglehold.

Other good and important English books and series were coming along: Ruth Teuscher's *Junior Drill Pads* from Racine, Wisconsin, the *Habits and Skills* workbooks by three marvelous lady English teachers from Cicero, Illinois, and of course the *Adventures in Literature* series was coming out a volume each year, 1929-32. In time, HB came to be recognized as the largest—and by many the best—publisher of high school English books in the industry. English was my own strongest subject and it was here that I needed the least outside advice. I was fortunate, too, in acquiring a number of talented teacher-authors with whom I could work smoothly and happily. There were, of course, a few flops, such as the *Pupil Activity English* series for junior high schools.

The success in high school English illustrates one of Alfred Harcourt's soundest publishing theories: publish from your editors' strength and interest, not just from calls of the market. The editor must *care*. He must be so involved that, for a trite example, he thinks about his project as he shaves in the morning.

After the English list came social studies and in the late twenties at HB that meant *Exploring American History*. In 1923, before I came to HB, Miss Mabel Casner, an unknown teacher from West Haven, Connecticut, brought a MS to S. Spencer Scott. It consisted of readings from a variety of historians and ingenious pupil activities: constructions, cutouts, map work, songs, games, and a dozen other clever things to do, which would help a pupil learn American history. SSS was attracted, negotiations poked along, and early in 1928 SSS secured at Miss Casner's suggestion the collaboration of Ralph Henry Gabriel, Professor of American History at Yale (next door to West Haven), and also currently editor of the Yale *Pageant of America*, one of the first heavily illustrated series of reference books in American history. This was a winning combination. Casner and Gabriel had several of the ingredients for success: Miss Casner knew the children, what they could and could not do; like a queen bee she could produce endlessly fascinating activities. Mr. Gabriel had the knowledge of American history, plus an instinct for the colorful, the interesting, the exciting episode, as well as a great experience with pictures and illustrations. Miss Casner's activities needed trimming, selecting, and ordering. Mr. Gabriel's writing needed most careful editing. It had the spark of life' but it had to be trimmed and firmed up. These jobs I could do. And Mr. Gabriel and I added some American folksongs, the first time any such thing had appeared in an American textbook. One ingredient was lacking: a new and exciting organization that salesmen could talk about.

It was Dudley Meek, by this time manager of the Chicago office, who supplied the crucial push toward the "Unit-Problem" approach which, when fully developed from Miss Casner's step-by-step "problem" approach, put the finishing touch on the book. DM studied one summer at the University of Chicago under Professor Henry C. Morrison,[1] who won him over to the "unit-problem" approach. For Casner and Gabriel this meant that the major divisions of the book each be oriented toward understanding a major development in American history instead of breaking the book into the conventional "parts" and "chapters." We found that by organizing the book around the big unit-ideas in American history, history as a mere memorizing of facts disappeared. Instead, the nine unit-ideas focused pupils' energies on the fundamental understandings of American history to be mastered. Each unit in turn was broken into a series of problems, as Miss Casner originally planned. Each problem represented a necessary step toward the understanding of the unit-idea.

Here, for example, is Casner and Gabriel's opening unit:

I. An Awakening Old World Discovers a Strange New World

PROBLEM 1. Why Did Europeans Wait 500 Years to Discover America Again?

PROBLEM 2. How Much Did the Early Explorers Learn about New World Geography?

PROBLEM 3. To What Manner of Life Had the Inhabitants of America Progressed by the Time the Europeans Found Them?

---

[1] *Morrison's great book* The Practice of Teaching in the Secondary School *(Chicago: University of Chicago Press 1926; revised edition, 1931) had a strong effect on* DM, *me, and many other* HB *people.*

Casner and Gabriel's *Exploring American History* was typical. The HB Textbook Department sought constantly to teach understandings, not the mere memorizing of facts. We had much success, but also much frustration, notably in two fields: government, where Magruder, published by Allyn & Bacon, held sway for decades, its monumental array of facts resisting our best efforts to displace it with a book of more penetrating understandings, *Government in Action* by Mary and Robert Keohane and Joseph McGoldrick (comptroller of the City of New York under LaGuardia); and biology, where Holt's Moon and Mann, with its encyclopedic chapters of fact laid end to end, outsold our good-selling *Exploring Biology* year after year. We tried to teach the big ideas, buttressed by facts, not the facts for their own sakes. After all, what is the residue of a course at school or college years later? A point of view, a changed attitude, an understanding built into the personality—these remain after "the facts" have faded into a gray dimness. And always we sought to use the "problem-solving" approach and arouse student activity.

After a great deal of work, Casner and Gabriel's *Exploring American History*, a big book in a red buckram binding, was published in the spring of 1931. It was not an auspicious time, as the Depression was well into its third year. Nevertheless, Casner and Gabriel had an impact; it began to sell, and, with many revisions it continued to sell through the 1960's. Most textbooks fade away after two or three revisions but Casner and Gabriel seemed to have a touch of immortality. Certainly no editor ever had more cooperative authors!

The Depression hit the Trade Department much harder than it did the Text Department. In fact, the Text Department was surging ahead with such a powerful up-thrust that only one year—1932, at the very depth of the Depression—failed to show an increase. I must say that Alfred Harcourt acted swiftly and intelligently early in the Depression. He cut costs, he trimmed personnel, he was strict with the Trade Department, but he steadily backed with funds and moral support the work of the rising Text Department. As a result my fortunes suffered not at all in the Depression years.

But intellectually the Depression had a powerful effect. It caught all of us by surprise and we were confused. We assumed that the prosperity of the twenties would go onward and upward without end. The Marshall-Taussig-Johnson brand of economics, taught in the colleges, let us down badly. There was nothing in our college courses or educational background that accounted for the floundering of the economy and the menacing steady growth in unemployment, the "Hoovervilles," the sellers of apples on the street corners. Wall Street had no satisfactory answers or explanations. Nor did the politicians or the administration in Washington. We read widely, we talked, we saw that the old guideposts pointed nowhere. There was a wide bankruptcy in economic and social matters. Small wonder it was that many turned to Marx, Lenin, and the Soviet Union, for here at least there were ready answers to the question, "Why is our economy in trouble?" Russia seemed immune to the Depression. Planning and socialism maybe held the answers. Or so many of us thought in the early thirties. Maurice Hindus and his eloquence—in writing and in lecturing—influenced us.

Probably for me the most valuable source of intelligence on the Depression and its time of troubles turned out to be an unexpected and surprising one: a discussion group established under the initiative of my friend Roger Baldwin of the American Civil Liberties Union. Roger felt the need for a free-wheeling discussion group and so called together about thirty young and middle-aged men at the Civic Club near Union Square, in April 1931. Most of us welcomed the suggestion to get together once a month and exchange ideas freely and off-the-record. We felt that we could learn much from each other and gain from the necessity of sharpening one's ideas in debate and discussion. We early agreed on the name, "The Dissenters," and the group, most remarkably, still carries on, meeting once a month from October through May, though none of the founding members and few of the old standbys who carried on our rip-snorting discussions through the Depression, New Deal, and war years attend any more.

There was always a good sprinkling of distinguished or well-known members:

ADOLPH BERLE, early New Dealer and later Assistant Secretary of State
WILLIAM NICHOLS, head of the magazine *This Week* for many years
CAESAR SEARCHINGER, radio commentator
MORRIS PARIS, Assistant Comptroller of the City of New York

ARTHUR GARFIELD HAYS and MORRIS ERNST, prominent lawyers

LADISLAS FARRAGO, author and correspondent for the London *Chronicle*

ROBERT BENDINER, author of books, columnist for *The Reporter* magazine, now working on the Editorial Page of the New York *Times*

AARON BODANSKY, bio-chemist, Russian-born, avid reader of *Pravda*

FRANK HERCULES, novelist and barrister from Trinidad

LISTON OAK, prominent Communist for several years

HERBERT HARRIS, New York teacher and technocrat

STEPHENSON SMITH, native American radical from the Far West

JOHN SCOTT, writer and assistant to the publisher of *Time*

ARMAND ERPF, head of research for Loeb, Rhoades, Wall Street broker

HARRY CRAVEN, ex-Englishman, printer, and publicist

OSCAR BRAND, singer, guitarist, and radio, TV, and Broadway performer

JACOB TRAPP, Unitarian minister who officiated at my second marriage

There was over the years a kind of executive committee, of which I was a member. It was a thinly disguised dictatorship of Roger Baldwin's. In addition to setting up the programs and choosing the meeting places, its main work was to maintain a good flow of members. We were pretty ruthless in discarding the inarticulate ones, those chaps who came and just sat, making no contribution to the discussion. We also tried to manage a variety of points of view, for a wide spectrum engendered colorful differences of opinion. We had little difficulty in recruiting from the left and the moderate center, but it was always a struggle to find and hold onto conservatives. And a true reactionary was more prized than fine gold! Actually, over the years Armand Erpf of Wall Street was our main and greatly valued voice from the right.

At first enough dissent just naturally flowed from the group and we depended entirely on ourselves. But pretty soon we found we needed the infusion of new views from guest speakers, sometimes one to a meeting but more often two or three representing clashing points of view. The format took shape early: dinner at a restaurant in Greenwich Village, preceded or not by wine or cocktails; after dinner, fifteen or twenty minutes for a presentation by each of the speakers of the evening, sometimes briefly interrupted by a doubting or disagreeing member; a period in which speakers answered questions from the floor; then, the juicy part of the evening, in which members could make speeches and air their views; finally, the summing up in which the chairman went around the circle asking each member to state briefly his position on the issue of the evening. Starting with dinner at 7:00 and the dissension at 8:30, the chairman would try to wind it all up by 11:00. One meeting—on the role of the Catholic Church, held during the Spanish Civil War when feelings ran high—went on until 1:00; and that was the only meeting where Roger Baldwin, our permanent chairman, nearly lost control and had to ask a member to leave.

Here José Calderon, a loyalist whose brother had recently been killed in the Spanish Civil War, confronted a de-frocked Benedictine monk, and a professor of law from Fordham University. They battled it out until José was thrown out.

Over the decades outstanding meetings had Adolph Berle on "How To Come Out of a Depression"; Lawrence Dennis, the American Fascist, but more respectably intellectual than most of the Fascist troglodytes; Bill Browder, the brother of Earl Browder, head of the Communist party; and (much later) William Buckley, the reactionary author of *Man and God at Yale* and (still later) Conservative candidate for Mayor of New York. There were many other notable speakers who came and talked to the Dissenters: Barbara Castle, Labor MP; Pethick-Lawrence, another Labor MP; Norman Thomas, in his articulate prime; Jay Lovestone, head of a Communist splinter group; A. J. Muste, the saintly director of the Fellowship of Reconciliation; Jimmie Carey, originally a member of the Dissenters and later Secretary of the CIO; and from the German underground came Hans Krebs, the author of a fantastic book, *Out of the Night*.

Out of the long and delightful experience of the Dissenters, always watchful for writing talent for HB, I got three good trade books: John Scott's *Democracy Is Not Enough*; Robert Bendiner's *White House Fever*; and Frank Hercules' *Where the Humming Bird Flies*. None of them were large sellers but neither were they losers and all three lent some lustre to the list. I tried hard in the early sixties for a fourth book, Roger Baldwin's own story, based on his reports of some eight hundred typewritten pages at the Oral History project at Columbia University.

Despite our best efforts and extreme urging, we at HB never could untie Roger from his reluctances. Hopefully, we even had one of the trade editors work for weeks, editing Roger's transcripts, and as a final heroic gesture had the MS set in galleys and sent to Roger to read, re-vise—and approve. But he didn't approve. Too bad. Roger had a great story to tell. Still has.

After George Shiveley left in 1928, the College Department rather languished. Under the unimaginative editorship of Francis W. Rogers, also an émigré from Holt, only a fair number of new books were published and none of them big sellers. I continued to do a good bit of college selling—Dartmouth, Harvard, MIT, and a few others—enough to keep abreast of collegiate needs and currents. Late in the fall of 1932 I came up with an idea which led to many things. The idea was essentially a simple one: to publish in one inexpensive volume all the reading for freshman English. It was an obvious transplant of the *Adventures* or *Literature and Life* idea of the comprehensive literature anthology from the high school to the college scene. It was admirably keyed to the times. Funds of freshmen and their families were scanty and anything that would reduce the costs of a college education would obviously have strong appeal. Only Rogers at the office was lukewarm in response to this idea, and I got the signal to go ahead full blast with *The College Omnibus*. Quickly I signed up James Dow MacCallum, my favorite teacher from the Dartmouth English Department, a satur-nine redhead in his thirties, to be its editor. He did the job for a flat fee of $1,000, which now looks pretty miserly and I guess it was. How-ever, the decision for a fee instead of royalties won me great respect in the office as a good businessman, a reputation that stood me in good stead over the years. The book was a bargain for the freshmen, but it also had about a dollar extra profit for HB built in.

I sometimes daydreamed about that "extra dollar." Suppose I offered to give up all other compensation from the Company and simply took a dollar a copy as my salary and commission. The first years of *The College Omnibus* it would have been a good-paying arrangement, for the book was a smash hit from its first year on and through eight edi-tions or revisions. As I remember it, the year 1933, the book's first year, brought in sales of about 30,000 copies—big stuff for those days and especially for a small publisher. A dollar a copy would have brought me over four times my annual compensation of those Depression years.

We knew that there soon would be competition for *The Omnibus*, and there was. But we also determined to keep well ahead of competitors, by means of an annual revision correcting weaknesses as reported from the field and adding new attractions to the table of contents. The major change in the *1934 Omnibus* was to substitute Thomas Hardy's *The Return of the Native*, his best novel, for *The Mayor of Casterbridge*. We chose the "Mayor" in the first place because it was considerably shorter than *The Return of the Native* and we felt we couldn't afford the space for the longer novel. We also updated the essays and strengthened the short story section. The *1934 Omnibus* was a bigger book but we kept the price the same—$2.75 list, a real bargain even in the depression years of low prices for everything.

With each edition we sought to come up with new and newsworthy features. In the 1936 edition, which I have always considered one of the best of all, we supplemented Dr. MacCallum with a distinguished board of contributors: Louis Untermeyer for poetry, Percy Marks for essays, among others. Each specialist contributed a lengthy introduction to his type of literature, explaining how to read, interpret, and enjoy it. The introduction to the essay was hardest, for it turned out that it is hardly a "type" of literature at all, ranging from the personal essay of Bacon, Lamb, and Christopher Morley, to a hodgepodge of magazine articles and other topical pieces for stimulating thought, discussion, and freshman writing.

There was one tragedy, or near-tragedy, in preparing the *1936 Omnibus*. At the Thanksgiving 1935 meeting of the National Council of Teachers of English in Indianapolis, I picked up the MS of the poetry introduction from Louis Untermeyer, who with Carl Sandburg was a featured speaker there. In Chicago I stopped off for dinner with my old college roommate, Norman Maclean, now a teacher in the English Department at the University of Chicago. After dinner we were invited to see the movies of the Chicago-Ohio State game at the home of Clark Shaughnessy, the University of Chicago football coach. We wanted especially to see the sensational running of Jay Berwanger, the greatest and last of the Chicago halfbacks. Unfortunately, I made the mistake of leaving my suitcase, with Untermeyer's MS in it, in Maclean's car. Upon returning to the car after the home movies, we found a brick had been thrown through the car window and my suitcase was gone. We reported the loss to the Chicago police, but there was never a trace of either suitcase or poetry MS.

Back at the office first thing Monday morning, I telephoned Louis Untermeyer in Toledo and told him what happened. "Excuse me," said Louis, "while I go to the bathroom and throw up." He had no carbon copy. But he then performed a remarkable feat: in the next two weeks while the content was still fresh in his mind, Louis wrote again the 10,000 word "Introduction to Poetry" for the *1936 Omnibus*. Of course we paid him a double fee.

We skipped 1937, for the 1936 edition was a great smash hit, and in 1938 brought out a true alternate edition, with a new crew of editors supplanting Dr. MacCallum. A new twist in 1938 was to transform the "essay" section into "a book of exposition," which we made available separately. It, too, sold well. *The College Omnibus: Eighth Edition* appeared in 1946 and by this time its sales had eroded and times had changed sufficiently that the clamor for another revision was too dim to be heard. But there aren't many college freshman books that sell for nearly two decades, or have so many imitators!

About this same time I had my first opportunity to buy some HB stock, an opportunity which I eagerly seized. Today the stock is worth over one hundred times what I paid. The dominating philosophy (AH's and Don Brace's) was never "to hog it all," but rather to share with the key people. Such a policy attracted, held, and stimulated good people over the years. However, as the Company grew larger and larger, it became more difficult to come up with formulae that would spur the individual key person to his creative best, yet not make the rewards too lush, and stay within a sensible and fair overall structure of company compensation. For example, at one point I had a commission of 10% of Text Department profits. If maintained, it would have in some later years brought me over $400,000—obviously a gargantuan overpayment. But the sharing principle was a good one and helped mightily to build the Company over the years.

In mid-1932 I married the creative and attractive novelist, Helen Grace Carlisle. Somehow, we all took it for granted that she would switch over her future writings from Harper and Cape & Smith to HB. As Alfred said, "She's a good writer and we want to publish her." I married, as it were, within the book industry and she did switch to HB.

For me personally *The College Omnibus* led to my being asked to become the editor of the College Department. I continued as editor of the High School Department and held both posts until 1954, when both departments had become so large that I had to give up one of them. And so in November 1932, at about the time of the first election of FDR as President, at the nadir of the Depression and just before the bank holidays, I happily took on the double editorship.

CHAPTER FOUR

UPWARD
AND ONWARD
(1932-1936)

THE BANK HOLIDAY IN FEBRUARY OF 1933 was surely the true bottom of the Great Depression. FDR had been elected in November of 1932 but little or nothing was done to stem the downward slide of the economy, or indeed the crumbling of the social order in the horrible three-month gap that then existed between the November election and the March inauguration. It's hard for people of the sixties to understand how close this country came to disintegration or revolution in the early thirties. Banks failed, farmers began to resist—with their shotguns—seizure of their land, unemployment reached nearly fourteen million, or more than one-third of the work force, the old-fashioned gold standard throttled our foreign trade, and the general bewilderment was paralyzing. All this we realized and talked about in the office, at lunch, at home, at parties.

Somehow, really serious outbreaks and general violence were averted, but the play of events was obviously moving to a grand climax of some sort. Then FDR arrived, like the oldtime U.S. cavalry in the Indian fights, just in the nick of time. His rallying cry—"We have nothing to fear but fear itself"—shook this nation out of its paralysis and FDR's famous first one-hundred days, the early formulations of the New Deal, stimulated the people to work for Recovery. We were roused up. There were new ideas, industry meetings, conferences, and parades. The spring of 1933 became a great time to live!

Along with practically all other industries, the book industry held meetings to figure out what we could do to speed Recovery. Alfred Harcourt, I remember, was one of the first to see that the book industry held little hope of cooperative or unified effort of any sort and he quickly pulled out of the NRA (National Recovery Administration) meetings. Nevertheless the publishers were, I believe, spurred by all the alarms and excursions to somewhat greater individual efforts.

In the Textbook Department we had a bit of an in, as Rexford Guy Tugwell, one of FDR's braintrusters, was a valued college author. His college text, *American Economic Life and the Means of its Improvement*, in collaboration with two colleagues in the Economics Department at Columbia, came out in 1931. It was one of the first texts to break the stereotyped and by now arid "principles" approach which continued to dominate economics, aptly characterized "the dismal science." The Tugwell book stressed institutions and attempted to present, describe, and analyze how economic affairs actually worked through the organizations, special arrangements, techniques, and groupings of men in America.

It early occurred to us in the High School Department that there ought to be a high school adaptation of this "institutional" approach to economics. We asked Tugwell to join in or lead a collaboration with a high school teacher in the preparation of this new kind of economics book. Dudley Meek came up with the high school collaborator: Howard Hill, of the University of Chicago High School, a nationally recognized social studies bigwig and author of Ginn's highly successful ninth-grade civics textbook. Also since Tugwell was a prominent New Dealer and in the eyes of some people a bit of a "leftist," Hill's midwestern conservatism was considered a proper balance. Under Meek's urging we even called the book the Hill and Tugwell *Our Economic Society*, putting Hill's name first. In the actual operation, Hill did little real work and Tugwell himself almost none. The author, or adapter, was Leon Keyserling (later chief Economic Advisor to President Truman), who had just emerged from his graduate work and elementary instructing in economics at Columbia to go to Washington as Tugwell's assistant. Keyserling pitched in, and Tugwell's third collaborator on the college book, Roy Stryker, a specialist in photography and the visual approach, contributed heavily. I, too, worked long and hard, and we put the book out in good time—early in 1934. It made a good start and was heading for a key adoption in Kansas City, when Dr. William Wirt, school superintendent of Gary, Indiana, made his famous attack on Tugwell and other New Dealers as "communist plotters." Wirt was sensationally headlined all over the country. Dr. Wirt's attack, though finally discredited, was a body blow to the book's promising start. While it made its way with modest sales, the book's sales were disappointing; it was an early casualty in the gathering attack on Roosevelt and the New Deal.

School people are timid people, especially in times of depression. Textbook publishers know this and so, unlike most other sellers and promoters, try to keep their product out of the news. Newspaper stories rouse up the fringe groups, stimulate aggressive parents, all of whom move in to stir up trouble for school superintendents and school boards. There seems to be no sensible or easy way in contemporary America to counter intemperate attacks on school materials. Most publishers and school people try to avoid conflicts rather than win them. There was never, at any time, any thought in the HB office of revising or modifying Hill and Tugwell's *Our Economic Society*.

In the middle thirties a good many publishers issued books which would illuminate the economic scene, broaden and deepen understanding of our economic problems, and explore the new trails being blazed by the New Deal. But HB by the greatest good luck—or good publishing instinct—had the most important author of solutions for the country's dilemmas: John Maynard Keynes, the great British economist, whose theories showed capitalist countries how to come out of depressions. Keynes had the answers that the economy needed; FDR applied some of them, and economics in the United States was never the same again. He was the father of "the new economics."

I met the enormously impressive Keynes only once, on his visit to this country in 1935, one day in Donald Brace's office, and I attended his lecture at the New School for Social Research. Later I asked DCB who was the finest mind in his whole experience, and without hesitation Don said John Maynard Keynes was. Throughout the years Keynes had been good for HB: he contributed one of the Company's first books, *The Economic Consequences of the Peace*, in 1919; he led HB to Virginia and Leonard Woolf and other members of the fertile

Bloomsbury Group; and above all he contributed his own great works of economic theory and less formidable, easier-to-read books of essays.

In these Depression years as the new Editor of the College Department, I began to enrich the college list. To serve as a supplement to the good-selling *College Omnibus*, I sought a freshman composition book to pin to its coattails. French's *Writing*, published under George Shiveley's auspices, had never really caught on, so that I felt free to seek a new entry in this fiercely competitive field. At this time—and really throughout my reign as College Editor-in-Chief—we made a great point of having only one entry in a field. We concentrated on one *Omnibus*, one freshman composition book, or one American literature for effectiveness in selling; but also such concentrated attention was a good argument in securing and holding authors. I compared our philosophy of college publishing to a high-powered rifle in contrast to the "shotgun" scatter of such rivals as Macmillan, or Prentice-Hall, which would publish two or three or more texts for a single course, all competing together and splitting the time, energies, and loyalties of their editors and salesmen. For a small publishing house trying to get ahead, my argument was often a winning one.

The freshman text I came up with was *Better Themes*, by Percy Marks, my old friend from the English Departments of Dartmouth College and Brown University and by now a highly successful novelist. His *The Plastic Age* was one of the landmark novels of the twenties. It had made a big success in the bookstores and the movies and he had followed up with other good sellers. I had met "Perk," as he preferred to be called, rather than "Percy," in the wee small hours at Scottie's Restaurant at Dartmouth. I worked the night shift there my freshman year from eight to one, first as a dishwasher and then as a waiter. Perk and "Pop" Hewitt (my freshman English instructor), usually came in about eleven for scrambled eggs and I always waited on them. Afterwards, in New York Perk and I picked up again and deepened our friendship.

Perk had great wisdom about writing and I learned much from him that I applied to the editing of textbooks. His violent antipathy to jargon ("case," "instance," and so on) infected me, too, and benefited many a sentence in our textbooks. I got Perk to write *Better Themes* for freshman English courses and *The Craft of Writing* for the more creative and advanced writing courses. Perk wrote the difficult Introduction to the Essay for the *1936 Omnibus* and began to work for me, when I needed him, as a free-lance editor and re-write man.

Editing a good editor and writer is a difficult and tricky business. And so it was with editing the MS of *Better Themes*. There were of course no elementary faults or difficulties in the MS; rather, Perk had made the mood and feeling of the work too *personal*, even a bit stiflingly personal. I felt there was so much "I" in it that many college teachers, themselves persons of strong egos, would not care to teach it. I strove to reduce, if not take out, the big "I," and enlisted the help of my wife, Helen Grace Carlisle, herself a sensitive writer. We succeeded in good part, for *Better Themes* came out and was a good, though not a big, seller. Too, it lacked a really adequate handbook section of grammar and usage, which was and doubtless still is the *sine qua non* of big sales in freshman writing courses.

There were at least two good college texts started by Francis Rogers and completed by me: *The Book of Living Verse*, edited by Louis Untermeyer, and *Major American Writers*, edited by E. E. Leisy, of Southern Methodist University, and Howard Mumford Jones, of the University of Michigan and later of Harvard. Jones was a great brain and he became a great friend. Though sensitive and quickly irascible like most red-headed men, Jones was instantly productive. Just lead him to a typewriter and good copy which rarely needed editing by his editor or even revising by himself poured forth. Through the years Jones and his quick-to-fire integrity were a constant check on my sometimes too commercial tendency. A gay and sportive man, Howard Jones, he and his good wife Bess gave the Reids many great times!

Another original enterprise started in these middle thirties was a two-volume typewritten economics text *Contemporary Economic Problems and Trends* by Horace Taylor of Columbia University. It had the "institutional" approach rather than the attempt to teach the outworn and discredited (so I thought) "principles" of economics. Horace Taylor assembled the materials, much of them strictly up-to-date, got the MS typewritten for reproduction, and we published it by offset in two volumes. It was "different" and made a dent all right, but it was too cumbersome (two big quarto two-column volumes), and much of its material too temporary ever to become a big seller. When finally we persuaded Horace to reduce it to one volume and to supply a larger portion of his own writing, rather than reprints of various kinds, the book did better.

And from City College of New York there was Morris Cohen and Ernest Nagle's *Introduction to Logic and Scientific Method*, one of the truly great and enduring textbooks of this century. (My editing of this one was miniscule.) There was excitement and fun in publishing these college books, keeping up with good minds and with the quick-moving times.

In the High School Department in the middle thirties I had a couple of frustrations and defeats. After the dismal failure of Werremeyer's *Cumulative Mathematics* in the late twenties I tried math again, this time a more powerful and sustained effort, with the aid of a general editor, Bancroft Brown, a fine and sensible Professor of Mathematics at Dartmouth. We worked well together and brought out two intellectually and academically respectable books: *Algebra: A Way of Thinking* by Professor Ulysses Grant Mitchell, of the University of Kansas, and Helen M. Walker, of Teachers College, Columbia, and *Plane Geometry and Its Reasoning* by Henry C. Barber, of English High School in Boston, and Gertrude Hendrix, a colleague of Barber's. Both books stressed the reasoning or thinking approach to mathematics and both were intelligently and skillfully written. Neither managed to catch on. One reason, I suspect, is that the timing was not right; that is, neither represented the kind of forward step in teaching that math teachers were ready for. Also, and perhaps just as potent, our salesmen did not seem to know how to sell math books, and we in the office did not know how to train them. They were good in selling English books, social studies, and even French books, but not math. Or Latin, which was the other notable failure. *The Beginnings of Rome* by Raymond Haulenbeck, of Newark, had an attractive idea: teach the traditional Latin grammar but use the history and culture of Rome as the content. We worked hard with Haulenbeck, and we published a good-looking book, which fell flat on its face.

It was otherwise in French. There again, I applied the "omnibus" idea. We gathered the reading for second-year French into one capacious volume, enriched by pictures, fresh selections as well as the stand-bys, and good editing by Arthur Gibbon Bovee, of the University of Chicago High School. *Aventure par la Lecture* was another smash hit for the middle thirties, a good seller in both high schools and colleges.

Bovee was an interesting character, discovered and advocated by Dudley Meek. A hard though somewhat careless worker, full of ideas, always needing advances against royalties, usually in domestic difficulties of one kind or another, Bovee called forth our best editorial efforts. It was a constant struggle to help him keep his personal problems from interfering with progress on his textbooks. Finally, we had to take the drastic measure of putting his personal finances directly under the charge of Dudley Meek, then manager of the Chicago office, who lived in the same apartment building with Bovee. It was an uneasy alliance, which Bovee characterized by saying, "Dudley is a good friend—in a cruel sort of way!"

But our efforts in French would have got nowhere if unexpected editorial reinforcements had not shown up in the office. Not from me, certainly, for I had squirmed under my five years of Latin and three years of Spanish, despite pretty consistent marks of "A." The fresh editorial talent in French came from Newbury LeB. Morse, my successor in the New England territory. After discovering that his French held up well and that he had the systematic meticulousness for good editing, sss and I not only fed him some work on French MSS but also arranged for him to spend a long summer in France, where he refreshed his knowledge of the language. As always, good outside textbook authors must have good editors on the inside. NLM worked with Bovee, Ramon Guthrie (a good poet) and George Diller (a good teacher) of Dartmouth, and that famous wit and poet of Cornell, Morris Bishop, well over the years to give HB a healthy beachhead in modern French. This position we held until the early 1960's, when I managed to secure for HB the Audio-Lingual Materials (the ALM), sponsored and developed by U.S. Government funds, in competition with seventeen other publishers. The ALM then enabled HBW to become the foremost publisher of modern language books for schools.

In these Depression years the Text Department recruited many of the good people who developed and contributed mightily to the growth of the business in the late thirties, forties, and fifties. Dudley Meek, I repeat, always had a fine instinct for talent. He hired many good people: Burnett Ball, rotund and powerful young public-speaking teacher who became the greatest textbook salesman of the mid-century years. Eventually as general sales manager, in the sixties he presided over a force of one hundred fifty salesmen and he personally won probably more state and big city adoptions than any other salesman of his times. Another of DM's powerhouses was Emerson Brown, who was teaching in Kansas. He joined HB (instead of going into educational research as he could have) and learned to sell books under DM's firm tutelage. After winning a couple of Kansas adoptions, his intellectual quality strongly showed and in 1935 it was agreed to bring him on to the New York office to edit social studies books. He had been pre-ceded by another émigré from East Erie Street (our Chicago office), Eleanor Fish who came into my editorial department as an assistant. While she was a maid-of-all-work—and a good one—she took over more and more the art, visual, and photography side of the editorial work. She became my first full-time editorial assistant, aside of course from secretaries.

Other significant additions to the staff were King Burney, beautifully fitted by training and temperament for the mild intrigue of state adoption work in Texas; Ted Purintun, highly intellectual but erratic, who did help on college editorial work; Sydney Stanley, one of the top college salesmen through thirty years.

It was SSS who was fundamentally and originally responsible for the great HB policy of recruiting its editors primarily from its own sales staff. Such a policy did much to insure the close coordination and full understanding which existed between sales and editorial for nearly four decades. In many ways I was, as editor-in-chief, the main beneficiary of the policy. I had direct access to the salesmen instead of having to rely on sales managers, who inevitably filtered out some of the raw stuff of which good publishing decisions are made. Salesmen and editors met as equals at sales conferences and slugged out their differences. And many a time one or another of the salesmen would invite me to travel with him for a few days in his territory, trips on which I always learned plenty and sometimes recruited authors and advisors. The salesmen also knew that an idea or a complaint would make a big noise in the editorial office. Finally, we just had a lot of fun together outside the formal and normal contacts of the office. Many were the binges, songfests, bridge games, dinners and lunches at exciting restaurants, and lengthy sessions of talk at or after sales conferences in New York or Chicago, or at educational conferences where HB staged exhibits in various cities.

For many years sss insisted that each editor do some selling on his own, that he have a sales territory as he himself had the high schools of New York City, the University of Michigan, and West Point. It was a fruitful policy, as the *Adventures* series bears witness. I had a bit of territory, diminishing in size as editorial requirements on my time increased through the thirties. But finally the requirements of the editorial job were such that I gave up all high school selling and finally in 1950, when my left leg began to go bad, I even gave up calling on Dartmouth, the last of my colleges. Other editors gradually gave up selling, too, and by the middle fifties the requirement that editors sell had all but disappeared. Too bad.

There were failures and abortions in recruitment, too. One of the most famous was the case of George Champion, who followed me in Psi Upsilon at Dartmouth by two years. George came in to see me on his jobseeking trip from Hanover in the spring of 1926. sss, a fellow Psi U, was much impressed and we offered George a selling job, the usual start. George had obvious qualities of personality and character but he turned us down in favor of a job in a bank. Eventually he became chairman of the board of the Chase Manhattan Bank, second largest in the country. One always wonders about "the road not taken."

My oldest friend, Gerald C. Wood of Denver, tried textbook selling under Dudley Meek, working out of the Chicago office, but didn't last more than a few months. Nat Finney, close friend of Lee Deighton and Ted Purintun at the University of Minnesota, became a legend at HB as the writer of the most literate and best sales reports ever submitted. After a few months DM did a bit of checking, found that a large percentage of them were fictional, and persuaded Finney that his undoubted talents would find more congenial scope in some other business. Nat became a newspaper reporter and ended up with one of the most respected bylines in the nation's capital, first for the Cowles papers and later for the Buffalo *News*. Holmes Boynton, son of the

University of Chicago's distinguished professor of American literature, Percy Boynton, tried several different territories, flashed in each one, but somehow lacked the staying powers and stamina a textbook salesman needs. And Frank Stutesman, a folk character out of deepest Indiana, was one of DM's most delightful failures. He always could sell lots of books when he worked, but he seldom worked. Once he came to the New York office and entertained us all summer long with his stories, wit, and charm, but finally and regretfully he had to go. Another of our most successful salesmen of "local color" was Elbert Eibling, with Pennsylvania Dutch credentials, who masterfully covered the tricky and difficult western Pennsylvania territory for many years and wound up finally as Eastern sales manager in the sixties. Another important new hireling in the office was a sales correspondent, Emmy Krohn, eighteen-years-old, beautiful with long reddish-brown hair, and one of the best letter-writers in the High School Department.

Dudley Meek it was who introduced sales meetings, which became great events of each textbook year. Arduous were the preparations by editors and sales managers. They offered the editor a chance personally to indoctrinate the salesmen and the salesmen a chance to blow off steam and indoctrinate the editor. Many of our best ideas for new books and ideas for revising books came out of these meetings, directly or indirectly. I always learned a lot and the salesmen always knew they had a sympathetic pipeline, direct to the editor. Well do I remember the first sales meeting, when Dudley arrived from the Chicago office at the head of his formidable invading force, all bulky, strong young men—Lee Deighton, Burnett Ball, Emerson Brown, Frank Moore, each of whom was loaded, primed, and ready to fire. Our New York office salesmen and editors were not so formidable but with the supporting force of SSS and me it suffered the invasion handily. The extra-curricular activities of eating around at some of the great New York restaurants, drinking together, playing bridge, and above all talking shop to and sometimes through the dim hours were best of all. Book salesmen have a great advantage over most other salesmen: their "shop" is the whole world of ideas and education and therefore utterly inexhaustible!

Our social life in the middle thirties was partly literary, but it was different from our previous social life in New York. For in 1934, my wife and I bought a house in West Norwalk, Connecticut from Anne Nichols, author of Broadway's long-running farce *Abie's Irish Rose*. We moved out of New York; we mingled in the social and literary life of Fairfield County. There was an HB enclave at Riverside, where AH, DCB, and Gus Gehrs (the trade sales manager), had built houses. We consciously avoided Riverside, preferring not to have a twenty-four-hour dose of office people. Ann Watkins, the literary agent, and Roger Burlingame, Scribner editor and writer, were in Redding. So was Stuart Chase. Robert Wohlforth, author of the anti-West Point novel *Tin Soldier* and now Treasurer of Farrar, Straus & Giroux, and his ex-newspaper wife, Mildred Gilman, also a novelist (*Sob Sister*), the great gypsy writer, Conrad Bercovici, and the humorist Ted Shane were in elm-studded Ridgefield. Ursala Parrott, of *Ex-Wife* fame, and her red-headed, nonstop talking friend, Hugh O'Connor of the New York *Times*, were in Wilton. So were Ted and Mathilde Ferro, writers of the best of all soap operas, *Lorenzo Jones*. Vera Caspary, author of *Laura*, successful as a book and as a movie, lived in Wilton part of the year. And John Hyde Preston, erratic author of *Revolution 1776*, a successful HB trade book, and his beautiful wife, Barbara, were in New Canaan. John was hard to keep on the beam, but with all his quirks, he never wrote a bad paragraph in his life. And Lowell Thomas not too far away at Pawling, N.Y.

The Bercovici clan had a big white house on the outskirts of Ridgefield, with a pingpong table on the big porch, where Mirel, the youngest daughter, took on and beat all comers. There was Rada, the romantic, dark-eyed eldest daughter, married to swarthy Speed Swigart, who was Danish, not Spanish, and Ghorki, the youngest and fiercely mustached son, and Rion, the reliable oldest son. At the head was Conrad, with the biggest mustache, the most talented of them all, with ample Naomi, his wife. Conrad was reputed to have originated as a gypsy in Transylvania, and certainly he had been in the midst of literary affairs here and in Paris for many years. He was a good short-story writer.

Once established in Connecticut, we soon developed what became a small tradition: the Harcourts and the Reids would always go to the Yale-Dartmouth game in New Haven together. In 1935 or 1936 I had ordered the customary four tickets to the game when AH came into my office and said, "Look, Gertrude Stein and Alice B. Toklas are coming out to Riverside for the weekend. So I guess we'd better call off the trip to the Yale game." I had a better idea, and suggested that we get two more tickets.

The two ladies from Paris were delighted ʳo swell our football party to six. Gertrude Stein hadn't seen a football game since 1902 and perhaps Alice B. Toklas had never seen one. Once settled in the huge Yale Bowl, after the usual picnic lunch and couple of drinks on the grass of the parking lot, Miss Stein was fascinated by the huddles of the two teams. She said, "Here's a typically American thing. The huddle is like the old Indian war dance: they get around in a circle and then dash off." During the half one of my drunken Dartmouth friends came up and offered Gertrude a drink from his flask, which she turned down, in a friendly way. She was a delightful person, and did most of the talking. Miss Toklas did not say much. This episode is written up in *The Autobiography of Alice B. Toklas* and it has been reprinted in several anthologies for colleges.

The nation's central business of the middle thirties was surely the organization and rise of the labor unions. John L. Lewis, head of the aggressive and comparatively wealthy coal miners union, was the man of the hour, with his beetling brows, his sober rotundity of voice and figure—a man of weight and substance. In action, he seemed like the fabulous Bronko Nagurski, irresistible fullback of the Chicago Bears.

The fever to get organized spread from rubber to autos to textiles and of course penetrated the publishing industry. Many of us felt in those exciting years that it was not only right for working people to organize and generate the power to better their lot but it was also right for the country to balance the economic power of the corporations with the economic power of organized labor. Organizing was the *progressive* thing to do. It would help the New Deal and the country, we thought. We approved the illegal but effective "sitdown" strikes.

HB was never a hotbed of labor unrest or excitement. It was still a personal sort of company and those of us who did get involved in trying to organize the publishing industry did so more out of intellectual conviction than out of economic unrest. AH felt (or I sensed, rightly or wrongly, he felt) that a young man like me should share in the intellectual enthusiasms of his generation and be a part of it all. Within limits, of course. DCB was more conservative and SSS, on the surface at least, sympathetic, tolerant, liberal.

About this time I discovered I had a small competence in addressing groups. It was fun to exercise this ability to speak and I had plenty of opportunity at the various organizing and regular meetings of the period. Bob Josephy, the book designer, and I were the chief people from HB and we were soon elected to the executive committee of what became The Book and Magazine Guild, a name, incidentally, which I suggested and which was quickly adopted. Soon I was elected as the first vice president of the Guild, a job at which I worked for about a year.

The president of the Guild was Jim Gilman, head of production at F. S. Crofts, a leading college publisher. Eventually he paid for his Guild prominence by losing his job. Two other impressive executive board members were David Zablodowsky and Al Taylor of Viking. David had a lovely mind, rich, learned, and deeply philosophical. Al Taylor was a Dartmouth man, son of a rich father on the Pacific Coast, the best organizer I ever saw in action—and a devoted member of the Communist Party. After a couple of years, when the Guild was well launched, Al simply disappeared, and I never did discover where he went or what happened to him. Another devoted, hard-working member of the Guild was Lillian Lustig, of Young Scott Books (juvenile book publishers). She served as secretary and was always an important cog in the Guild.

These were the days of the United Front. We believed, I believed, in the working principle that we could collaborate successfully with anyone who shared the same objective. Like so many positions in political life, this one was partly right and, as it turned out, increasingly wrong. We did work together successfully in setting up the Guild, for example, and the Communists among us were no more than the hardest-working minority. Many people in many organizations worked with them. Roger Baldwin and his Civil Liberties Union worked with the Communists until about 1939. In addition to the Guild, I participated in the League against War and Fascism and some other United Fronts, usually aware of the Communists' role and confident I could maintain my independence. Finally the course of events shattered the various United Fronts and the hidden collaboration of the Communists on executive boards and on committees became so obnoxious that I had to revise my old working principle and admit that I couldn't work with Communists any more.

But earlier, in 1936, came the real parting of the ways for me. It was then that I, along with Dudley Meek, was offered a post on the Board of Directors of HB and I had to choose—management or employee. Obviously, I couldn't work on both sides and, without any internal conflict really, I opted for management, resigned from the Guild as officer and member, and became a director of the Company. Thus ended my brief career in the labor movement and thus began nearly 30 years as one of the top executives of HB. An end and a beginning!

The birth of my first son, Jamie, led directly to my first and only encounter with Thomas Wolfe, the gigantic novelist of the thirties. Right after Jamie made his entrance into the world at a small private hospital at 60th and Madison, I saw that he and his mother were both fine. It was about eleven on that fine summer night of July 10, 1935 when I was swinging along on the wings of the evening, an exultant young father full of the joy of his first-born. Suddenly a giant of a man—he seemed seven feet tall and fifty axe-handles wide—stepped in front of me, utterly blocking my progress, and said, "Give me a light or I'll kill you!" With shaking hand I lit his cigarette and ducked swiftly under his arm and down the street. I'm sure it was Tom Wolfe, for he was definitely in town that night, he was full of liquor, and it was the weird sort of thing he was thoroughly capable of. This, I thought, is at best one sort of contact with the literary great!

These were strenuous times for me—with the building of the college list, the close editing of the high school MSS, learning and inventing editorial routines and techniques, a vigorous social life, helping organize the book and magazine industry, and long hours at the office. There were successes, yes, but also some defeats and frustrations.

Throughout this busy period athletics was a great safety valve. I had tried and enjoyed the usual boyhood sports: football, baseball, basketball. And I'd developed through the YMCA and various private exercises a good strong body with enough athletic skill to play on the scrubs on the East Denver High School basketball team. But the scrubs in basketball was my peak, until I learned handball, went to Dartmouth, and in my senior year won the college championship in handball singles. Handball was indeed a minor sport and if any of the truly gifted major athletes had been free for handball I'd not have become champion. However, I was quick, full of stamina, and had a good punch in both hands—the requisites for good handball.

In New York after college I found it difficult to make good arrangements for handball, so that I shifted over to squash tennis. It is, in my view, the ideal metropolitan sport. Courts are available in mid-town Manhattan to most college graduates. A busy young man can get a great workout in a half or three-quarters of an hour. The action is so fast and the ball in its green net cover travels with such speed that the game is hard to excel for sheer excitement. It can be played well into a man's forties, whereas handball or even squash racquets (much the same as squash tennis but with a slower ball) require the bottomless reservoir of physical energy of a man's twenties or early thirties. Finally, it's a perfect game in which to take out on the fast-traveling ball a day's accumulation of irritations and minor frustrations. After a good match on one of the beautiful squash courts on the thirty-third floor of the Hotel Shelton, where I mainly played, I'd arrive home in early evening easy in body and mind. At the Shelton I won our local tournaments several years and enjoyed playing with Barrie Sullivan, the hotel pro, a slightly wild but altogether charming Irishman. The best I ever did was to get to the finals of the national Class C championships in 1940, where I lost to a man from the Harvard Club. Handball, squash tennis, and later golf, indoor tennis, and bowling were safety-valve, physical conditioners, and above all, great fun through the years.

My modest athletic competence also contributed a grand versatility. In college intellectual interests took the primacy and the world of books and ideas became most important. But one can't read, discuss, write, and intellectualize all the time. Sports form the great counterbalance.

There's a danger of ostracism for the boy or young man who is thought "too bookish" by his fellows. My enthusiastic participation and modest ability in sports were sufficient to keep me from being labeled as a grind for getting good grades and for an interest in things of the mind. Thus, I was able to be active in two worlds and to maintain a versatile life.

CHAPTER FIVE

THE HONEYMOON YEARS

(1936-1942)

I ALWAYS THINK OF MY EARLY YEARS in the upper echelons of HB as the honeymoon years. Power struggles and hard crises were deep under a smooth surface of growth and success. For the three new directors —Hastings Harcourt, Dudley Meek, and me—there was the excitement of learning about hitherto hidden aspects of the Company, its profits, its expenses, the salaries and commissions of all (including AH, DCB, SSS) advances, sales, successes, failures—the whole works.

True, there had been a bit of a struggle upstairs in clearing the way for Hastings. I didn't then and don't now know the full story, but clearly Gus Gehrs, the trade sales manager and one of the originals to leave Holt and cast his lot with the new Company, was pushed out to make room for Hastings. He sold his stock, a fairly sizable chunk, for which he received a good big sum. He used it to purchase control of Womrath, the chain of bookstores in New York City, which he ran for many years.

The Gehrs ouster was one step in the growing alienation between AH and DCB, once the closest of partners. It was not only Gehrs' going but the entry and elevation of Hastings in the Company that marred the relationship. Early on, the two of them had promised each other "no nepotism," for the thrusting of the Holt boys into Henry Holt & Company in the teens by Henry Holt had frustrated AH and DCB and had hurt the company. Don had only daughters, Kay and Donna, whereas Alfred had one son. But all this was under the surface, glossed over, in the honeymoon years of our directorships.

It became our custom to meet for dinner at one of the directors' houses in Westchester or nearby Connecticut. We would start in the fall at AH's house, then DCB's, and so on down the pecking order to the newest and youngest of the directors. After cocktails (a modest number, always) we'd sit down to dinner, with the hostess of the evening the only woman present. Then after dinner AH would preside over a most informal and delightful meeting. Discussion was free but there were few if any serious disagreements aired. We examined "the figures" and the elder statesmen talked for the edification of the younger men. A bit later we prepared and presented reports and plans. For example, I prepared a report on editorial plans and prospects for the College Department and Dudley Meek prepared one on sales plans and prospects for the High School Department. After much talk the meeting would end and people would drive off home. These informal dinner meetings occurred with regularity and replaced the most irregular and even more informal meetings of the earlier Board of Directors, which had as members in addition to AH, DCB, and SSS, our lawyer Melville Cane and Gus Gehrs. At our meetings, Hastings as secretary kept good minutes and the whole operation was a more formal and massive one. An underlying intention, I believe, was to train and sophisticate the younger echelon in terms of Company-wide, not merely Department-wide responsibility.

The context for the growth and success at HB this second half of the thirties was nationwide economic recovery, spotty but nevertheless strong; the disheartening course of the Spanish Civil War; the looming menace of Mussolini's Fascism in Italy; the terrifying, cancerous spread of Nazism in Germany; the ineptitude and mesmerized paralysis of Britain and France in the face of these challenges; the growth of the Red Army despite the endless bloody "trials" and internal convulsions in Stalin's Soviet Russia—all topped by FDR in his heyday with the New Deal at its brightest. Even the debilitating struggles between FDR and "the nine old men" of the Supreme Court only slowed and did not stop the splurging New Deal.

My sympathies of course were with the Loyalists in Spain. Their long-drawn-out but gallant struggles against forces too great for them made for a long emotional drain on sympathizers like me. I was, as it turned out, half-right and half-wrong about the Soviet Union. I was right in judging that the Red Army in the desperate final clutch had the strength to withstand and eventually, with our help, to stand off Hitler's gigantic military machine. But I hung on stubbornly too long to my confidence in Stalin and the Communists.

The "long march" of the Chinese Reds, romantically presented by Edgar Snow, gave me a lasting interest in China, an enduring mistrust of Chiang Kai Shek, and the durable confidence that Japan could never conquer. Here again, I was half-right, half-wrong. The Chinese Reds were strong and finally won out; but their revolution seems to have turned into a nationalist drive for empire. It would be a supreme irony if William Randolph Hearst's "yellow peril" of 1910, discredited for lo! these many decades, should become a reality at the end of the century.

In 1937 King Burney, our Texas man, asked me to come to Texas to help him in the final five weeks of his drive for the seventh-grade history adoption. I was pleased and complimented at this visible evidence of respect by sales for editorial. Furthermore, I expected to learn at first-hand about state adoptions, which account for about a third of the school textbook business in the country. All my experience had been in states considered "open territory," that is, states where adoptions or the ordering of schoolbooks is left up to the local units.

New England especially, where I had had the bulk of my selling experience, was renowned throughout the textbook industry for the "chickenfeed" nature of its book ordering. The locus of decisions about which textbooks to order varied from town to town and even from school to school. School boards and school board members rarely had anything directly to do with ordering; in some school systems it was the superintendent who picked the books; in others, the principals. In most open-territory high schools, the department heads had the largest say and in large high schools a wise and industrious textbook salesman would try to see not only the principal and department heads but also the experienced teachers who often advised and influenced their department head. The larger cities usually had an authorized textbook list from which each school could order. A few cities had formal adoptions, but local option prevailed in most of the open territories of the East, North, and Midwest.

Texas was the largest of the state adoptions, which characterized textbook ordering in the South and Far West. It was in the thirties even more desirable than California, which for many years printed its own state-adopted elementary textbooks by renting the plates from the publishers. This practice seriously cut down the size of the business—and the profit—and some publishers would not get in the running for California's business and permit their plates to be rented. For many years sss kept HB from going after California "plate" adoptions. So . . . Texas was the big plum, the most wanted adoption of all. Up through the eighth grade, ordinarily Texas would adopt a single "basic" textbook for a single course and order a copy per pupil to be used over a five-year period. In grades nine through twelve, usually a multiple list was adopted; that is, for each course five books were listed and then the publishers of those books had to mount a second campaign over this largest of all states, calling on as many of its twelve hundred high schools as possible. Once a basic book was adopted by Texas it got all the business in that course; no further selling effort, with its attendant expense, was necessary. The seventh-grade American history adoption that King Burney and I went after would produce sales of 150,000 to 180,000 copies over the five-year adoption period. This was the big time in textbook selling!

We had prepared thoroughly and well in advance for the Texas history adoption of 1937. We were at this time making a general revision and up-dating of our Casner and Gabriel book. We changed its title from *Exploring American History* to *The Rise of American Democracy* for the 1938 edition. For the Texas edition we persuaded Miss Casner and Mr. Gabriel to take on a Texas collaborator, A. W. Birdwell, president of the Stephen F. Austin State Teachers College at Nacogdoches. This intelligent Texas educator advised on the MS of this mid-thirties revision and wrote a few passages about the Alamo and other topics dear to the hearts of Texans. He also was a shrewd advisor to us on the political infighting of the adoption—and he was an honest man. King, I think, somewhat over-estimated the value of Birdwell's contacts and ties with Texas Board and adopting committee

members, when it came down to "the nut cutting" as the Texans color-
fully phrase it. But without his name on the title page we would have
stood no chance in the adoption. Our most feared competitor had distinguished authors: the head of the History Department at the University of Texas (Dr. Barker), Dr. Dodd (our Ambassador to Germany
in the thirties), and Professor Walter Webb, also of the University of
Texas, famous for his theory that the invention of barbed wire and the
Colt revolver won the West for us. But their book had the handicap of
having had the seventh-grade adoption for several years and it was
considered by some to be an "old" book. Many Texans were tired of
it. A fresh new book usually has a certain advantage.

I went by train to Austin, the capital of Texas, (planes were considered a bit risky in those days) and King met me there in mid-Septem-
ber. His campaign had been going since mid-spring, but now for the
next five weeks we staged our big push to the final decision by the
Texas State Board of Education in mid-October. King quickly briefed
me on overall strategy. We were single-shots for the big adoption; that
is, we were submitting a bid on only one book, the Casner-Gabriel, in
order to avoid a deal at the last minute in which we would get a minor
adoption or listing. King had decided, wisely I agreed, and so did
Dudley Meek as sales manager, to go all out for the big one. King and
HB, we figured, win or lose in the fall of '37, had a long future in Texas
and we determined to play the game like the people of weight and con-
sequence we believed ourselves to be.

Immediately, King and I had lunch with Gent Sandiford, an Austin
lawyer, new on the Board but the one whom King figured might have
the skill and strength to stand up to and possibly outmaneuver the
other "strong man" who, King figured, was committed to our chief
rival, the Barker-Dodd-Webb book. There was much talk at lunch,
none of it at the realistic, hard-hitting level yet. Later we saw Mrs.
Sandiford and paid her our most gallant attentions. King was intent
on missing no tricks. As I discovered, much goes in these adoptions on
personal contacts, personal interest, and personal attention.

Soon that first afternoon we were in King's Buick, a big comfortable
car in which he indulged himself since he drove almost constantly, on
our way to East Texas. There we would see Dr. Birdwell, the Texas
collaborator on the Casner-Gabriel, and get his advice on adoption

tactics and contacts. On our way we stopped off in Tyler and spent a delightful hours with an old friend of King's, who had just retired from the Board of Education, an old time Texas character full of local color. We sat in the sun on the main street, told stories, and talked for an hour. Nearby were many younger men, squatting on their heels, a typical Southwestern pose, as they passed the time of day. I was glad to have this enjoyable hour of Texas talk and flavor, though I doubt if it forwarded our cause very much. We got to see Dr. Birdwell, a tall frontiersman sort of man, late in the day in his office.

Our immediate task was to interview all members of the Textbook Committee to make sure that our book was among the five the Committee was to recommend to the Board and from which the Board was to make the final choice of one basal text. King was pretty confident Casner-Gabriel would be listed by the Committee but he wanted it to be their Number One choice, a real though not compelling advantage with the Board. We had appointments with the Committee but their geography was widespread—from Orange near the Louisiana border to Lubbock far to the west and north in the Panhandle, a thousand miles apart.

One interesting afternoon we took a Committee member who enjoyed a bit of gambling and quaffing from the dry county in which he lived (Texas had local option of liquor) across the state line into a wet and gambling county or parish in Louisiana. The gambling house we went to was run, appropriately enough, by the "Lawless boys," gambling brothers who sat in on what seemed to be a perpetual stud-poker game. King and the committee member and I agreed to pool our winnings or losses; primarily, King had warned me in advance, because our guest was not a very good poker player, and of course we didn't want him to be a big loser when he was our guest. As it turned out King played well and won some money, I about broke even, and our guest did lose. The three of us together broke even, but we'd had some good drinks, a fine dinner, and a lot of fun. Such a situation was open to abuse, as money might have passed hands under the guise of poker "winnings."

In other ways the long drag and hard work of the adoption was broken. Our longest drive was from San Antonio starting about five in the evening, 800 miles to Lubbock, where we arrived about four in the morning. With two of us driving, shifting every hour, and stopping for coffee or a stretch every two or three hours, we made it comfortably. I remember one piece of absolutely straight highway, 70 miles long, which we made in precisely one hour. Texas jackrabbits, which flashed across in front of the car, were the only hazards. Checked into our hotel for about three hours sleep, we got up at seven and drove out a bit north of the town for some fine dove shooting; that is, King did the shooting. I don't shoot, never have, but I enjoyed the expedition. We delivered our dozen or so doves to the cook at the hotel and had some of them for a delicious breakfast next morning. Good eating, in the early American style!

So it went: long drives, long discussions of the political infighting as we cruised; talks with Committee and Board members and their advisors at schools, or their homes, rarely over a drink; painstakingly building our case for Casner-Gabriel; culminating in the preliminary climax, the formal presentation to the Committee in sessions assembled, preparatory to the final big climax before the Board of Education a week later in Austin. The presentations by representatives of about fifty companies on the eight or ten book adoptions of that fall took about a week at the sizable town of Temple, Texas.

Altogether there must have been in Temple about a hundred Texas bookmen and their supporting forces: editors (like me), sales managers, authors, and others from the higher echelons at the home offices. King himself made the main forty-minute presentation of the Casner-Gabriel, with a few supplementary remarks by me, followed by some questioning, mostly friendly, by members of the Committee. All this took place within a context of extra-curricular activity during the week, mostly with the other bookmen. We talked, played bridge, talked, did a little horse-trading, talked, and played golf and had a few drinks. There were some high-stake poker games but King and I avoided them. We had one very exciting golf game which reached its peak on a short, par-three hole. It was Harcourt Brace vs. Houghton Mifflin, a keen rivalry as there was an underlying touch of unfriendliness between King and a little Houghton Mifflin man, built like and resembling a jockey. No unfriendliness with Jimmie Hopper, the top HM Texas salesman, who later became their general sales manager. The match was even as we came up to this short hole on a high tee looking down on a postage-stamp green. I led off with a grand shot which ended up a couple of feet from the pin, a sure two for a birdie. Then the little jockey-type HM man stepped up and made a hole-in-one, one of three I have witnessed in forty years of golf. My two lost out to his one! Many years later I made a hole-in-one, playing at Waccabuc in Westchester County with Emmy, my wife.

Of course we did no hob-nobbing with our chief rival in the history adoption, although King had always been on good terms with their two men. But friendships with rival bookmen were put on ice during adoptions. At last the long week at Temple drew to a close and both Casner-Gabriel and its rival were on the list of Committee recommendations. The show packed up and moved ninety miles south to Austin for the showdown with the Board the next week.

But the Board required only three days and its members were, for the most part, incommunicado, while the final wheeling and dealing went on. King made the presentation to the Board and did a good job. We marshaled all our strength with Gent Sandiford as anchorman, but we lost. On the final day, the secretary of the Board appeared at the top of the steps outside the Board room in the lobby of the Hotel Driskill; he finally read off the seventh-grade history decision. The history adoption went to the rival we had feared all along. King and I quietly made our way back to our hotel room and within an hour or so we killed a fifth of whiskey between us. The liquor had absolutely no discernible effect on either one of us and later in the afternoon we checked out and drove the 250 miles to King's home outside of Dallas, where we licked our wounds. Back in New York, I mistakenly gave the story of the adoption to the education editor of *Time* magazine. It was a one-sided story, with some unfortunate implications about state adoption procedures and our competitors and it made some trouble for King. A year later King received a 100,000 copy adoption of our ninth-grade speech book and I always figured that it came in part to balance King's loss of the seventh-grade history adoption. But the *Time* story shook King's confidence in me a bit and I was never again invited to help in a big state adoption.

It was in this period of the middle thirties that our High School Department at last got a foothold in science. Earlier, our science offerings had been limited to rather trivial books of questions and problems in physics and chemistry and other supplementary, not basic, textbooks. Herein lies an important distinction: a basic text, when adopted or ordered, usually means a copy per pupil, whereas a supplementary book is limited to orders for single copies for the library or, at most, to orders in class sets; that is, one set of thirty copies or so that is used for reference and often shifted from class to class. The big business lay in publishing basic texts.

Early in the thirties, Frank Moore, our silver-tongued Ohio representative, discovered that the biology teacher in Salem, Ohio was not satisfied with any available biology textbooks and was writing and mimeographing text materials for her own classes. He gained her promise to consider sending me a revised edition of her mimeographed text. She did send it to me in the New York office. I read it with growing interest, even excitement. For the lady could *write*. Her science was sound and she clearly was a great teacher. I was particularly impressed by her treatment of two of the toughest and touchiest topics in high school biology: sex and evolution. I wrote her and indicated we wanted to work with her in producing a basic text in biology.

The lady's name was Ella Thea Smith, middle-thirties in age, short-haired, and a former Quaker. She had lost her formal religion in her exciting encounter with biology and evolution at the University of Chicago, but she retained the noble Quaker moral characteristics of forthrightness, mild non-aggressiveness, and clearheadedness over an underlying layer of iron integrity. I had encountered this Quaker combination of character traits before—in J. Russell Smith, the great geography author—and had learned to respect it.

I felt at first that Ella Thea should have a collaborator, a college teacher or experienced biologist. She agreed, and I tried a couple of big names at Yale and Harvard, without success. Finally we fixed upon John W. Ritchie, successful science writer for the World Book Company, a man in his fifties and a good talker. He and Ella Thea worked together at his farm in New Jersey one summer. She came on with her devoted husband, Marion Cox (an experienced and able illustrator and photographer). The Smith-Ritchie collaboration produced a good bit of ms. However, the collaboration fell apart and the basic difference between them was submitted to me. It was not an easy decision. Both wrote well, with an edge to Ella Thea. She wanted to present vertebrate and especially mammalian reproduction and evolution with no holds barred, while Ritchie, with his experience at World, was wanting to compromise, to play it safe. Finally, I decided to back Ella Thea and her concern not only for the integrity of biological science but also for her determination to tell the truth to the students. Furthermore, she was the active, practicing teacher—and a good writer—whereas Dr. Ritchie was the retired writer, living mostly on his royalties.

So it was full speed ahead with Ella Thea. We both, I think, worked the harder because of the rift with Ritchie.

Exploring Biology by Ella Thea Smith incorporated several "firsts" in science textbooks. We modeled its organization, like Casner and Gabriel's, on the unit-problem approach of Morrison. We took the nine biggest ideas in biology for units (verified as biggest by our outside advisors, a group of top college biologists), which were subdivided into problems, each of which became a step toward mastering the unit idea.

Even more revolutionary was the system of Technical Vocabulary Control which we worked out and used for the first time in any high school textbook.

Authors of biology textbooks—and other science textbooks for that matter—had felt free to incorporate into the MS whatever technical terms, and as many of them, as the subject seemed to demand. Sometimes the author would define the term and sometimes not. And so each textbook had in it a large and formidable science vocabulary, as strange and difficult to the high school student as the vocabulary of a foreign language. It happened at this period that I was carefully following the work of my associate Newbury Morse in his editing of Bovee's *Un Aventure par la Lecture* and other French books. Newbury was paying great attention to the Van der Beke Word List in French. It was the consensus of Van der Beke, his fellow researchers in language teaching, and experienced French teachers, that 1200 words was about the right load, the maximum of new French vocabulary that high school students could be expected to master in the first year of French. Foreign language books of the thirties and subsequently were all influenced by Van der Beke and did a better job for it.

We now asked ourselves how heavy a load of science vocabulary was *Exploring Biology* thrusting on tenth-grade high school students, these fifteen-year-olds. We spent several weeks on a careful count and analysis of the biology vocabulary in our MS and we found it used 1200 scientific terms, each of which needed defining just as much as one of the French words on Van der Beke's word list did. In short, we were asking students to master a "foreign language" (the biological science words) *and* the whole subject matter of biology, with its concepts, its laboratory work, and all that! As a check we ran analyses of the two high school biology texts then leading the field and discovered that each presented a vocabulary burden upwards of 2,000 science terms.

Heroic measures were called for—and taken. Ella Thea and we in the office agreed to try to cut the load to 600 terms or fewer if it could be done without diluting the science content. Then, just as important and perhaps even more so, we could concentrate full attention on the 600 surviving technical terms and systematically help students to master them. Here are the working rules we evolved:

1. Do not retain a term unless it is used at least three times in the book.
2. Italicize a term the first time it is used, pronounce it, and define it right then and there.
3. List it under the heading "Science Vocabulary" as the first exercise or activity at the end of the chapter, for review and testing.
4. List it again in the Glossary at the back of the book with a page reference to its first appearance and quick access to the definition, in context.

Thus we hoped to give the students a firm hold on essential terms, the labels and handles to the essential ideas in the course. As it turned out, this vocabulary control went over big with the biology teachers and gave our salesmen a great talking point. They could not only point with pride to our reasonable vocabulary demands (600 terms) but undermine the competition by attacking the absurdity of their 2,000 terms. This was comparative selling at its best.

Finally, we decided to go all out in teaching evolution. We devoted a whole unit to evolution as Ella Thea and I, and our advisors, the college biologists, wanted. We did not hesitate to use the name "evolution" in a straightforward way. The custom in those biology texts which did not completely ignore the idea of evolution was to call it "development" or some other synonym that the editors thought might be inoffensive and innocuous. Furthermore, we did not hesitate to present evolution, not as a mere "theory," but as one of the great foundations of biological science. In going so much further in presenting evolution than was the tradition in high school biology books of the thirties, we felt we were giving up all chance of state adoption business in the South and West and only a slim chance in Fundamentalist centers in the Middle West. But in compensation we hoped so to strengthen the appeal of *Exploring Biology* to true science-minded and forward-looking teachers that we would more than make up our losses in the open and less hidebound territories. It never hurts to get the best and most intelligent teachers on your side!

Soon after publication in 1938, *Exploring Biology* rewarded our decisions with good, substantial sales. We got the citywide adoption in Detroit, biggest city adoption in the country, and a little later it was listed and ordered in Atlanta, Georgia, much to our surprise and delight. The book's success was further dramatized when it upset the advance dope by winning state adoptions in Oregon and Kansas! Sometimes integrity does triumph over opportunism.

Another first: in the early forties *Exploring Biology* was the first to give the full and scientifically accurate account of race. It was based on the great pamphlet "The Races of Mankind" published during World War Two by the American Anthropological Association. Here again we probably gained more than we lost as the Negroes became better organized and acquired greater impact in the schools. But we were determined to present the best available science, let the chips fall where they may!

Exploring Biology went on through six revisions as one of the bestselling books in the field, usually second to Holt's text by Moon and Mann, which came on strong in the forties and fifties. In the sixties, sales of both *Exploring Biology* and Moon and Mann were substantially reduced with the publication of three biology texts sponsored by the Federal Government and the professional associations of college and high school biology teachers in the great educational revolutions of the sixties. Just before retirement, I played a decisive role in getting for Harcourt, Brace & World, the "yellow version," the best-selling of the three government-sponsored books. But Ella Thea and *Exploring Biology* remained my true loves over the years.

Right on the heels of the success of *Exploring Biology* came another one, to help establish HB as a serious contender for the business in science in the secondary schools. In the late thirties there arrived in our editorial office, through Ranie Burkhead, our hard-working Pacific Coast stalwart, a promising, lively MS for the high school health course. It was written by Jessie Clemensen, a teacher in a Los Angeles high school. We read it with interest, which came to a boil, when my colleague, Emerson Brown, whose main work was editing social studies books, had the brilliant idea of expanding the material to cover safety, as well as health. This would require a collaborator for Mrs. Clemensen, who liked the idea when we broached it. She suggested we approach Dr. Ralph LaPorte, nationally-known head of physical training at the University of Southern California; he was highly regarded in health and safety education circles throughout the country. Dr. LaPorte was willing. Not always by any means did a "national reputation" guarantee good work, but he turned out to be good and he and Mrs. Clemensen made a good team.

After several years work we published *Your Health and Safety*. It became an immediate success, for most schools liked the inclusion of the safety chapters. Having both health and safety in one book was an economy and a convenience; it enabled many schools to meet the legal requirements of teaching safety, which existed in a number of states, but was considered an awkward nuisance by many administrators. Soon the competing health books had to add safety material. As usually happens, the innovator gets the credit and gains the most. The imitators and followers do in part protect their holdings and lose less than they otherwise would.

There was only one really tough decision in the course of editing *Your Health and Safety:* how to handle the touchy area of reproduction and sex. Schools varied in their attitudes. The progressive ones wanted a straightforward, scientifically sound treatment included as a regular part of the course. Such a treatment coincided with our own predilections. But in some school systems teachers and administrators were confronted by a scool board regulation which forbade any teaching of sex. If such material were included, the book simply could not be listed or ordered. Clearly we had to furnish the material in a form which permitted the individual school freedom of choice. The solution was to publish a separate booklet, *Life Goes On*, of 36 pages in the same format as the textbook itself, which could be adopted and/or ordered separately. In *Life Goes On* were two chapters, one on the biology of sexual reproduction and the other on "the facts of life," both coolly, straightforwardly, and honestly presented. Sales of the booklet, over the years ran to about one-eighth of the sales of the basic textbook *Your Health and Safety*.

In the middle thirties enrichment of our editorial resources came from overseas—Vienna, to be exact. Into the office one day came a handsome young man, with just a touch of accent, named Rudolph Modley, and he represented a small organization he had just founded: *Pictorial Statistics*. He was the star understudy of Otto Neurath, the great Viennese chartmaker and statistician, and he had come to America to introduce Neurath's vivid ways of presenting statistical information. I was quick to find places in our textbooks to use Modley's know-how and talents and HB was the first textbook house to have his pictorial statistics. Our business relationship became a friendship; I got to know his equally talented wife Helen Post, and we worked together for many years—until Rudolph got a bit too expensive for us.

The big news in the College Department in these years of the middle thirties was the hiring of John H. McCallum (no relation to James Dow McCallum of *College Omnibus* fame). John had graduated from Harvard at the depth of the Depression and had taught at a private school on Long Island for several years. He came in to see me in 1937, seeking an editorial post, through our mutual friend Lindsay Todd Damon, Scott Foresman's great old editor. It did not take long for me to sense the quality of John McCallum and to offer him a job. He added great strength to our College Editorial Department. He fell at once in with the idea of doing some selling—and turned out to be a top salesman as well as a top editor. He was so hard-working and ambitious that he was seen on some of his road trips to run, not walk, from appointment to appointment across the college campuses.

John McCallum was of great editorial help, especially in English and history. We were trying hard to strengthen our history list in those years. Its backbone since 1923 had been *A History of Europe*, by Ferdinand Schevill of the University of Chicago, who had written its first edition in 1899. AH had taken the book over from Scribner, when Charles Scribner had expressed discomfort that Schevill espoused the then unpopular view that the guilt for World War One was not exclusively German. HB did well with it, revising to keep it up to date about every five years. On the average, its sales were second only to Hayes (Macmillan). One always knew when Ferdinand Schevill was in for a conference, for his great voice and hearty laughter would boom through the whole office. We called him "The Chief," as he was the founder and first head of the History of Civilization course at the University of Chicago, where my friend and old college roommate, Norman Maclean, was on his staff.

To know The Chief was to know integrity. His book had not only integrity but also the balance, shape, and design of a work of art. The final pinch came in 1946 when The Chief, approaching eighty, made his last revision. I tried to get him to take on a younger man as a collaborator who would then carry on further revisions. No, said The Chief. World War Two had ended Europe as Schevill conceived it and he felt his book should come to an end, too. Modern Europe had emerged about 1500 A.D., developed over four and a half centuries as a group of clashing nation-states, which had spread European civilization and their various dominant empires across the world. After 1945 Europe was overshadowed by the two new super-powers, Soviet Russia and the USA, and Schevill knew they forced a new design on European history. His wisdom prevailed. Schevill's *A History of Europe* is still in print and still used in some colleges, but its story ends with the end of Europe in 1945. The Chief was a great one.

The history list grew as we struggled manfully. One of the high spots was the vast two-volumed *History of Western Civilization* by Harry Elmer Barnes, a controversial scholar from Smith College. A remarkable man, with a touch of screwball. At one time he had a farm in upper New York State—with four Rolls Royce automobiles on it. He had the longest bibliographies ever turned in at HB, but there was nothing phony or padded about them. He had read all those books, for he was one of those high-powered readers who could let his eye run down the middle of the page and yet understand and retain what the author was saying. Barnes was not only a recognized historian (by some, though not all), but he also was a sociologist of some stature. At any rate he wrote his huge history of civilization (about a million words in all) and I edited it. It had a good sale in its early years but soon lost out to a smoother, less controversial two-volume offering by Scott Foresman. Ironically, it was edited by young Donald M. Stewart, who became the best social science editor in the industry. Fifteen years later we grabbed him for HB and he spearheaded our rise to the top in social studies in the fifties and sixties.

Entering our college list in the thirties were some other good books. Albert A. Trever's two-volume ancient history, sound and scholarly, made its modest, steady contribution year after year. We had two "Europes since 1815," neither of which reached the top. Erik Achorn, a gnarled, tough, and unyielding loner, wrote *European Civilization since 1815*, a spottily brilliant book that was one of my early editing jobs in the College Department. It was difficult editing, for he was a difficult man. The book had a great, notable first: it was the first college history to give real space to the Soviet Union and especially to the bulldog grip of the Communist Party on the government, which Achorn exposed brilliantly and ruthlessly. The other "1815" history (by Gillespie of Penn State) we took over from Knopf, at John Mc-Callum's urging, when Knopf for the second time broke up and sold his college textbook business. Dr. Gillespie was a large man, shy and timid. We had slow going with his somewhat dreary book, though it was sound enough.

Another character among our history stable was the ex-Englishman, Sydney Brown of Lehigh, whose medieval history I inherited from the Francis Rogers regime. Sydney had a lust for life, for whiskey, and for professional football. We were great New York Giants fans together, notably at the legendary game on ice at the Polo Grounds against the Chicago Bears. During the first half both teams were utterly frustrated by the icy field, especially Bronko Nagurski, the greatest of all fullbacks until Jimmy Brown came along for the Cleveland Browns in the late fifties. The Bronko's cleats did nothing but spin in the first half, as did all the other cleats. Then the Giants changed to basketball shoes between halves and literally ran away from the Bears in the second half, thereby proving that quick wits are better than bull strength even in professional football.

But John McCallum really won his spurs late in the decade by discovering and signing up Frank Chambers for our contemporary history. John read and was impressed by Chambers' *War Behind the War*, a history of the home fronts in World War One, published by our Trade Department and a good book. John discovered that Chambers was a Professor of History of Architecture, a brilliant young Englishman, teaching at McGill University in Canada. He went to see him and found that Frank was indeed interested in contemporary history and would like to write a book for us. At John's urging, we signed him up, got him two collaborators—one good one and one not so good— and they started furiously to write. Frank and Christina Grant of Stanford were finished on schedule, but the third collaborator wasn't. So Frank pitched in and did his chapters, too, finishing up in a succession of eighteen-hour days in the HB office right after Pearl Harbor. He did finish *This Age of Conflict* in time to meet the need for a good history of the world since 1914 for use in the Air Force training courses in the colleges early in our war effort in World War Two. John's first coup!

In college books we made some progress on other fronts, among them sociology. Earlier attempts under Shiveley and Rogers had not made much of a dent. But the Lynds' *Middletown*, published in the twenties as a trade book and in its text edition used in a variety of courses, had a richly deserved following. I had an idea, part of my policy of keeping good books up-to-date and trying never to let them die, to bring out a revised and updated edition of *Middletown*. I went to Robert Lynd with the idea, found him reluctant to touch the original book, but willing to return to Muncie, Indiana (Middletown) with a small crew and see what had happened in the ten or so years of boom and depression since the original survey. *Middletown in Transition* was the result. It had a good trade sale and a good and long-continuing sales in the colleges as a textbook. Today, in the sixties or seventies, why not a *Middletown Fifty Years Later?* Robert Lynd and his gifted wife Helen were wonderful people to work with, and the performance of their son Staughton Lynd, who fought in the forefront of opposition to the Vietnam war in the sixties, shows that the streak of idealism in the Lynd family has not thinned out.

In English, our major field of publishing, we were far from idle. We put Untermeyer's *Modern American Poetry* and *Modern British Poetry* together into one "Combined Edition," a real bargain, text and trade. I persuaded Louis to collaborate with Carter Davidson on *Poetry: Its Appreciation and Enjoyment*, a good but not really big seller. Davidson went on to become a successful and enduring college president. I have always felt deep down that it was our publication of this book that kept us out of the running for Robert Penn Warren and Cleanth Brooks' *Understanding Poetry*, one of the truly seminal textbooks of our times published by Holt. Normally one of our editors, their old friend, would have had enough strength with Brooks and Warren that their MS would come to us. *Understanding Poetry*, a brilliant piece of textbook writing, showed students—and teachers, too—how to read a poem closely. They followed up with similar books in fiction and drama and thus gave a new direction to the whole course of literature teaching, first in the colleges and eventually in the secondary schools.

One of our successful innovations was to introduce the technique of the symposium to big college textbooks. We did it first with *The College Survey of English Literature*, in which we signed up a specialist to prepare the MS for each of the seven periods into which English literature is customarily broken. This approach had many advantages. It was easier to sign up a top authority to write up his specialty than to ask him to spread himself thin over many periods, some of which he would have to refresh himself on. With many hands working, the job could be done quicker. And the sales advantage of many big "names" was not to be discounted. The danger in any multi-authored project is that one or two or three fail to come through on time—or at all. Still, safeguards can be built into contracts. One thing we found that made our proposal attractive to authors was a good-sized fee for each contributor in lieu of royalty, thus taking the risk for the author out of it, with a bonus after a certain sales figure had been reached to retain some of the more lasting sharing of success provided by royalty. The way for such a multi-authored project as our *College Survey* had been paved by other publishers who had collaborators of up to three authors—with signal success.

After much preliminary work in the office with both editors and sales people, I found myself on the road early in 1939 to sign up the seven collaborators for *The College Survey*. This was my first trip which did not also involve some selling, as well as MS seeking and scouting for authors. It worked out well and thereafter I simply went on "MS trips" in which the exclusive focus was on editorial matters. As I remember it, I signed up all or practically all of our first choices for *The College Survey*—and the work was soon started. The two gigantic volumes (2,312 pages, approximately 2.3 million words) came out in 1942. They were the fortunate receivers of the great monotype work and low prices of T. Morey & Sons of Greenfield, Massachusetts. (Printers too seldom get the credit they deserve!) Soon we issued a Shorter Edition in one volume and through the years *The College Survey*, in its various incarnations, has sold extremely well. It is still in use in the colleges.

Sometimes, in an effort to spot a trend and be the first to supply text materials for a new kind of course, I fell flat on my face. In the late thirties, the salesmen reported a gathering interest in introductory courses in the humanities. Columbia, Chicago and Minnesota had pioneered and now other colleges were wanting to try to develop humanities courses. Soon a promising project showed up: a mimeographed text, *Earning Our Heritage* by Professor F. E. Ward of Macalester College in Minnesota. It looked good to us in the office; it had been tried out and revised at Macalester and used in some other small colleges; Ward wrote well and showed imagination. To "play it safe" I persuaded Professor Edmund H. Booth of the Dartmouth English Department (one of the best "close editors" I've known) to join Ward as collaborator. They worked smoothly and hard together, with a colleague of Ward's, Grace J. L. May, for several years and produced two good-sized and intellectually respectable volumes. But this worthy project never got off the ground. Hindsight indicated two probable reasons: too much of the teaching success depended on Ward's "method," highly successful at Macalester where he was English head, but allergic to most college English teachers, who didn't want any "method" but their own. Oddly enough, I think high school people might well have bought Ward and his method, but not college folk. Also, too much of Volume Two was taken up by the reprinting of the whole of Thomas Hardy's vast novel, *The Return of the Native*.

A few years later I tried again for a big humanities offering and again was frustrated—this time by Dudley Meek, who simply lost his nerve. Following the success of *The College Survey* in its two-volume edition, I managed to stage a big conference, in our office in New York, of the chiefs of the three most prestigious humanities courses in the country: Mark Van Doren of Columbia (great teacher and poet), Clarence Faust of the University of Chicago (later with the Ford Foundation), and Albury Castell of the University of Minnesota, brilliant young philosopher. Dr. Faust brought with him his right-hand man in the course, my old roommate, Norman F. Maclean. We conferred for two days and if our confidence and sheer bull strength could have been maintained we could I think have pulled it off and got—in not too many years—two great volumes which, I still think would have enabled a great many colleges to install a sound humanities course and HB to have pioneered another big-selling and important project. But DM, by this time, had grown powerful enough to put on the brakes, and I had reluctantly to call it quits.

A lesser frustration but nevertheless a definite disappointment came with the publication of *Present Tense*, edited by Professor Sharon Brown of Brown University, another one of my great Quakers (J. Russell Smith and Ella Thea Smith being the other two). *Present Tense* represented our attempt to meet the recurring complaints against the various editions of *The College Omnibus* for their sheer size and heft. The world of college texts wasn't ready, we thought, for paperbacks (Pocketbooks hadn't made its breakthrough at the time) and so we experimented with soft, cloth bound "small" books, three of them in an attractive box. The selections were good, Sharon's editing tops, but the format turned out to be a handicap. The sales were substantial but for a freshman English book essentially disappointing.

Dudley Meek had come on from Chicago early in this period to become general sales manager, first of the High School Department and then of the College Department, too. We worked well together these years and the power struggle, which we both recognized was there, stayed under the surface. Dudley, I think, was disappointed that Emerson Brown, whose transfer from the Chicago office and entry into the editorial department Dudley initiated, did not stay or become his ally or partisan. Emerson was—and remained throughout his time at HB—his own man, not Dudley's or mine or anyone else's. I remember Emerson in his first week at the New York office at 383 Madison Avenue asking as we stood at the elevator going out for lunch, "Who is the dynamic little man with the mustache?" I replied, "That's Alfred Harcourt!" Thus, Emerson preserved his fiction of being "just a country boy from Kansas." During these years Dudley demonstrated that he was a good picker of people by building a strong staff of salesmen and a good staff of girls in the office to back up the salesmen. In Chicago Lee Deighton, Dudley's successor as manager, likewise was building, building.

About this time in the mid-thirties Ray Everitt, whose appearance in the Trade Department I had so envied when we both began in 1924, pulled out and went over to Curtis Brown, the literary agent, and then to Little, Brown in Boston where he eventually became executive vice-president. It continued to irritate Ray, I think, that he never could beat me at squash tennis when we occasionally played at lunchtime at the Yale Club. Dudley Meek, too, always was bothered because he could not beat me at either tennis or golf, the two sports we had in common. I never did really discover why Ray left HB. Perhaps it was just a better opportunity, or such a simple thing as more money!

Two very able young men replaced Ray Everitt in Trade Editorial: Charles A. (Cap) Pearce and Sam Sloan. Cap had one of the quickest, most knowledgeable, and richly intuitive minds I have ever encountered. He was a superb editor, our main contact with that rich lode of writing talent, the *New Yorker* magazine, but he could be moody and recklessly outspoken when he was full of liquor. And a trade editor in the thirties had his arm twisted frequently. Sam Sloan, despite a residue of physical infirmity from infantile paralysis, brought real magnetism, a great human warmth, and fine judgment to the Trade Department. Neither was really simpatico with Hastings, now in charge of sales for the Trade Department, and so both tended to consult DCB more and more and AH less and less.

Soon Cap and Sam were supplemented by another able young man, Chester Kerr of Yale. Chester wore horn-rimmed glasses and was quietly literary and intellectual. After four good years of trade editing he pulled out and eventually became head of the Yale University Press. Two other good young people shoved ahead in the late thirties: Helen Taylor and Keith Jennison. Helen, a rangy blonde, started in our College Department as a correspondent but soon was grabbed for bigger and better things by Trade. Keith came in the late thirties from Vermont. Both pulled out about the time of the big fracas in 1942, joined William Sloan of Holt in starting his own Company, and wound up eventually with Viking. Keith made a great innovation in the sixties with his large type editions for poorly sighted people.

It was in the late thirties that Alfred Harcourt began to slow up. He stopped working as hard as he normally did, to talk more and to do less. This change was precipitated, I have always thought, by the scare he received at Johns Hopkins. There was the threat of cancer in the urinary tract. Alfred spent weeks at Hopkins, and found a great doctor and surgeon who at least stopped or slowed down the onslaught for fifteen or so years. Like the true publisher he was, AH got his surgeon to write his autobiography and HB published it. Alfred came back from his ordeal in Baltimore courageous but shaken, and he was never again the powerhouse of old.

It was in 1939 that AH approached me and suggested that I switch over from text to trade and become editor-in-chief of the Trade Department. He envisioned that Hastings and I would together run the department and that I would have a pretty free hand to shape the editorial policies and decide the kind of book to publish. He painted an alluring picture of the interest and excitement of trade publishing. Here, it seemed, was my original publishing dream about to come true. Of course I was both complimented and deeply interested. But I had started so many projects in both the High School and College Departments and had made so many commitments to good people and true that I was genuinely whipsawed. I told AH how I felt and said that I would do whatever the Board of Directors thought was best for the business. And that was the last I ever heard of this proposal of AH's.

I have always thought that when Don Brace heard about the proposal he went to, or hurried up his negotiations with, Frank Morley of Faber and Faber in London. For not long after that Frank returned to the US to become a director of the company and Editor-in-Chief of the Trade Department. I was not at all unhappy, for I had many great text projects on the fire.

Shortly after Frank took over, Cap Pearce and Sam Sloan pulled out to form, with Charlie Duell of Morrow, their own publishing company, Duell, Sloan and Pearce, exclusively trade, no textbooks. Each of the three contributed some authors and talent, and Duell and Sloan, both of some independent wealth, put up the money. Their company became a success, though dealt a heavy blow by the accidental, sad death of Sam Sloan in the mid-forties. Their departure—and of Chester Kerr, Helen Taylor, and Keith Jennison—left a large gap in Trade Editorial and Publicity at HB.

Frank Morley added some distinction to our Trade Department. He was the younger brother of Christopher Morley, then at the peak of his literary career, and of the oldest brother, Felix, editor of the Washington *Post*. They were three large-framed, pipe-smoking literary brothers and Frank was the largest of all, really a huge man. He was a good writer as well as a good editor, with a certain combative quality. I had first met Frank at a hard-drinking cocktail party in Cape & Smith's old brownstone on 47th Street in 1929. Late in the party he and I terminated a verbal duel by throwing highballs in each others' faces. Diplomatic relations did not suffer, however, for later that summer on my first trip to London, Frank took the afternoon off from his publishing office and took me on a tour of the wine cellars of London—a delightful time!

Among the good authors Frank brought to HB was Simenon, then regarded mainly as a fabulously productive writer of detective stories but today considered to be a major novelist. For publicity Frank invented a new rum cocktail which he called "the Maigret" after Simenon's famous detective. Saroyan was another top Morley author. James Gould Cozzens was one of the great trade authors who started in the thirties and continued right on through the sixties, getting better and better. Through brother Christopher, Frank had a good connection with the Book-of-the-Month Club and that ended up, in November, 1941, in a "first" for me and the Textbook Department.

Some months earlier, through Sydney Stanley, our knowledgeable northeastern college salesman, I had got track of an unusual little book, published in an experimental edition, called *Language in Action*, by a young American college teacher of Canadian origin but of Japanese descent, S. I. Hayakawa. It was a brilliantly written introduction to semantics, at that time a new and exciting subject. I read it with growing excitement, knew we had to publish it, though it fitted none of the conventional textbook slots, and pronto, put in a long distance telephone call to Hayakawa, who was teaching then at the Illinois Institute of Technology. It was a good thing I did act swiftly, too, for Hayakawa said he was just entering negotiations with another publisher. My enthusiasm must have been convincing, as he finally said "Yes" in that first long telephone conversation. We did a careful job of editing, with the experienced and expert help of Percy Marks, and put the MS through the works rapidly.

I gave Frank Morley a set of proofs of *Language in Action* to read in hopes of a trade edition, and he found it so exciting that he persuaded brother "Kit" to read it, too. This led to the book's becoming the Book-of-the-Month Club's choice for November, 1941, the first time a textbook had ever received that honor. The book sold extremely well over the years in the colleges, but the trade and B-O-M sales were foreshortened by the onset of Pearl Harbor, which in turn led to a crisis with a happy ending for Hayakawa.

The Monday morning after Pearl Harbor, Hayakawa told me, he came to his eight-o'clock English class at Illinois Tech most fearful of what might happen. This usually articulate and fluent teacher was all tied up; he just stood in front of the class. The tenseness was broken by a little, red-headed freshman in the front row, who said, "It's okay, Professor, let's go," and the class and the professor came to life for a good class session.

In other useful ways Text and Trade worked together. We in both High School and College Departments were always on the alert to publish and actively promote and sell Textbook Editions of trade books of enduring value. For example, in the thirties, we brought out a high school edition of Sinclair Lewis' *Arrowsmith* and it soon became one of the comparatively small group of modern novels suitable for class study in high schools. A Text Edition of Paul de Kruif's *Microbe Hunters* found a steady market in both science and English classes. Steffens' great *Autobiography* came out in one volume and at the lower list price permitted by the smaller bookstore discount on college books sold vigorously for many years, mostly to freshen English courses. In addition, the High School Department published a shorter edition of Steffens, containing only the early chapters and a few of the muckraking ones from later chapters in the book. This tradition of text editions of the good trade books, which I happily carried on, continued through Saroyan, Dorothy Canfield, the Lynds, and many others.

December, 1941 brought warfare not only to the United States, but also to Harcourt, Brace and Company. Directors' meetings had been tapering off and the glow of hospitality dwindling. Finally AH decided to go all out. He not only proposed that Hastings be made head of the Trade Department but insisted on it. He encountered resistance. Helen Taylor and Keith Jennison were summarily fired by a.h. Dudley and I were upset and deeply disturbed, for we knew we didn't like the proposal and we had such doubts about Hastings' staying powers that we could not accept him as trade head. Frank Morley was, of course, against the move, as he would be definitely subordinated to Hastings. Don Brace was quiet. Dudley and I decided to talk it all over with sss.

sss was the balance of power if the struggle reached the ultimate showdown of a vote by the stockholders. The Harcourt family and the Brace family each held 39% of the common stock, the voting stock of the company—and sss held 12%. This was the iron triangle that dominated—and haunted—the inner councils of the company for a dozen years. But we all, especially Dudley and I, hoped to avoid a showdown and we worked for a compromise.

We approached sss and had a long discussion with him, discovering to our relief that he, too, not only lacked confidence in Hastings but also disliked the pressure AH was bringing to get his way. We gave sss our assurance of support in his opposition to the Harcourts. These were weird days at the office: little informal huddles in the office of one or another, long discussions at lunch, and a never-ceasing tension. I made a personal pitch to AH but didn't budge him a bit. Finally sss approached Don Brace and discovered as we had felt all along that Don was strong and solid in his opposition to the Harcourt proposal.

Finally, AH made his biggest move: he said he would retire from any active role in the Company and go to California, unless we gave in and let him have his way. He was surprised and disappointed, I am sure, when even the threat of the loss of the chief founder and longtime kingpin did not bring us around. We stood fast and in the heat of this struggle a new leader came to the fore: Don Brace. There followed weeks of haggling over the terms of AH's retirement and the final terms were indeed generous ones, as intended. AH and Hastings did pull out and go to California, where they settled in the beautiful small city of Santa Barbara. The rest of us returned to the office, where great heaps of work had piled up. Our private war was over, and so were the honeymoon years.

CHAPTER SIX

TO THE UPLANDS

(1942-1948)

AFTER PEARL HARBOR AND FDR's magnificent, eloquent response to it had united the country for a tremendous war effort, we at HB considered what we might do best to help. There was in the office or, indeed, in the country literally no doubt, no cynicism, no internal struggling over the necessity to win. Many of our good young men in the Textbook Department—Elbert Eibling and Norman Hunter from the New York territory, and others among them who, strictly speaking, were beyond military age—joined the military. Younger men of obvious talent and future, like Charles Murphy and Richard Manatt of the Chicago office, were vulnerable to military service and soon were off for training. I was an even forty-age and in good physical shape but I figured my optimum use was staying right on the editorial job. Altogether we lost a number of good men to the armed forces.

My response to the war was an editorial one: I proposed we publish a quickie entitled *America Organizes to Win the War* to help bring the schools into the war effort. This book was a symposium with a distinguished cast, headed by Vice-President Henry A. Wallace, and it included such notables as:

JOHN CHAMBERLAIN, book reviewer of the New York *Times*
HENRY STEELE COMMAGER, the historian
DAVID CUSHMAN COYLE, the economist
PAUL DE KRUIF, one of HB's good writers
LADISLAS FARAGO, Hungarian writer

AN ADVENTURE IN TEXTBOOKS

Dorothy Canfield Fisher, the famous novelist
Charles H. Judd, the educator
Prime Minister Churchill
Secretary Wickard (Agriculture)
Waldemar Kaempffert, *Times* science writer
Max Lerner, political scientist and (later) columnist for the New
York *Post*
S. L. A. Marshall, the writing Army General
Frederick L. Schuman, Professor of
International Relations at Williams

I had the idea for the book just before Christmas, 1941, quickly gained the approval and consent of my colleagues, and on Christmas Eve got on the long distance telephone to sign up the collaborators. The first one was Henry Wallace, who answered the phone himself! He said "Yes" right away and with him solid it was easy to get the rest.

Most of the writers I approached, caught up in the early war excitement and wanting to do something to help, said "Yes" and started work at once. For we had imposed on ourselves the "impossible" schedule of writing and producing this 395-page book in two months! With the remarkable speed of the writers, quick editing in the office, good outside editorial help from my old standby Percy Marks for re-write and from Professor Erling Hunt of Teachers College, Columbia, for social studies content, and—not least—heroic service from Plimpton Press's skilled and experienced corps of craftsmen in composing room and press, we did it. *America Organizes to Win the War* was published on March 19, 1942, just eleven weeks from gleam in the eye to finished books. It got into the schools all right, quick sales of some 20,000 copies, but it never became a smash hit. However, the experience of close working together with Erling Hunt led to important developments.

The colleges were quickly switched from their normal academic life to training tens of thousands of soldiers for the Army (ASTP), the Navy (NORTC), the Air Corps, and the Marines in various academic or technical subjects. Soon the Federal Government was ordering certain college textbooks in large quantities for the training effort in the colleges. I have told earlier how Frank Chambers worked eighteen to twenty hours a day in our office finishing his contemporary history,

This Age of Conflict, so it could be used in one of the Air Force courses. Our economic geography by Klimm, Starkey, and Hall was in great demand. And so were the authors, for geographers were really needed in Washington, especially for the war in the Pacific. But it was the publishers of technical books—McGraw-Hill, Wiley, and Prentice-Hall—that hustled the really big sales during the war. As publishers mainly of books for the liberal arts curriculum, HB benefited, but modestly.

The years of American participation in World War Two were years of high morale and considerable idealism. We never doubted the U.S. would win and we were practically unanimous in believing we were doing the right thing for ourselves and the world in bringing the downfall of Hitler's Nazi barbarism in the West and Tojo's brutal grab for big empire in Asia. It had been the same, though perhaps less intense, in World War One and later in the support of the United Nations' effort in the Korean War. There was substantial unity and firm belief in the rightness of our cause and some idealism. Very different from the divided nation in the Vietnam War of the sixties! Nothing approached this great united effort until the Moon-Shot of July, 1969.

Life and textbook selling in the schools went on during World War Two without much change. The big event in the fall of 1942 for HB was the Texas adoption in high school literature. Our *Adventures* series was put on the multiple list with four other series, most feared of which was Scott Foresman's new series, replacing their pioneering *Literature and Life.* But there was a proviso, namely, that we convert our four volumes from their small, single-column format to the more ample two-column layout. The Texas Board of Education allowed only one month in which to make the changeover! Maybe they thought it an impossible job within a month.

I had long been the leading advocate in the office of the single-column format, which I viewed as close as we could get in looks to books of literature which students encountered in bookstores and libraries—a view shared by many teachers of literature. Dudley Meek and some of the salesmen favored the more ample but less conventional two-column format. sss had been siding with me in this difference of opinion but the Texas opportunity brought him over to double-column. I came over, too, on the theory that we would offer two editions—the single-column and the two-column—and let the sales figures determine which the schools preferred. As it turned out, the schools preferred the two columns about two to one and in the 1947 edition of the *Adventures* series and thereafter, we published only the two-column format. Actually, the two columns of *Reader's Digest* and the ever-increasing acceptance of big two-column books in text and trade by the middle forties had made earlier resistance to it (including mine) seem a little silly.

Richmond Mayosmith, the gallant gentleman who was head of Plimpton Press, shared in our discussion of the Texas dilemma. Finally, he said he would turn loose the full force of his composing room working day and night on the tremendous job of resetting the four *Adventures* anthologies in two columns. He guaranteed he could do it in the month available, provided we would allow him to do the whole job inside the Plimpton plant, no proofs to publishers or authors; in short, no long lines of communication to slow down this speed job. Plimpton did it! We airmailed the official copies to Austin in time to beat the Texas deadline, and the two-column *Adventures* books were listed at last. Then Dudley Meek and King Burney organized a troupe of our best salesmen from all over the country for the multiple-list selling. King was a good organizer and a good instructor in the folkways of Texas schools and we walked off with the lion's share of the literature business in the 1200 high schools of Texas. All this helped to get the new administration under President Donald C. Brace and Vice-President S. Spencer Scott off to a great beginning.

I always think of 1942 as pivot year for the *Adventures* series. For the first time it led Scott Foresman in sales and never again, while under my aegis, was the *Adventures* series headed in the competition for the literature business of secondary schools of the nation. Scott Foresman, I always considered, made a great strategic error in abandoning *Literature and Life* for their new series, but of course this was not clear for several years. Dudley Meek brought great pressure to bear on the desirability of our developing another literature series as insurance against the *Adventures* fading away. I resisted for awhile and finally put together an alternate four-book series, the *Living Literature* series, under the leadership of Luella B. Cook, the great creative English teacher from Minneapolis, and Tremaine McDowell, talented and quirky professor of American literature at the University of Minnesota. The series had a spark, but only the tenth-grade book, under the skillful hand of Walter Loban (of Minnesota and Northwestern), ever showed signs of becoming a big seller.

In the meantime the *Adventures* series, my true love, was gathering new talent and strength which would keep it at the top for another twenty years. In the early forties we added good new *Adventures* editors:

MARY RIVES BOWMAN, of the State Teachers College at Commerce, Texas, an able writer, sage teacher, and that almost unheard-of creature, a true Texas liberal. She was recommended by King Burney. I never knew King to come up with a poor recommendation. Over the years one of Mary's great services was to mediate between the prejudices of Texas and the prejudices of the rest of us. It was always fun working with her. Mary worked on two levels: seventh and eighth grades, and on *Adventures in American Literature* at the eleventh grade.

WILBUR SCHRAMM, founder of the Creative Writing School at the University of Iowa, later head of the University of Illinois Press, and finally Director of Communications Research at Stanford, one of the most vari-talented men I have ever known. He was a good athlete with the lightning reflexes of a third baseman (actually he played a bit of professional baseball), a talented short-story writer, a great teacher, a fertile man of ideas, and in later years a leading producer of valuable reports for big foundations and the government.

BLANCHE JENNINGS THOMPSON, English head at Benjamin Franklin High School in Rochester, New York, editor of *Silver Pennies*, an enduring anthology of poetry for children published by Macmillan, and revised by Blanche in 1967, still going strong now in her eighties. She was a fine writer, who knew and loved the kids, and she became one of the strong members of the *Adventures* team.

NORMAN FOERSTER, English head at the University of Iowa, a leading scholar and writer, a man of impenetrable integrity who stayed with us for only one edition in the early forties.

WILLIAM ROSE BENÉT, distinguished poet, by this time working on his second edition with us. Bill told me his earnings from the *Adventures* series were greater than those of any of his other books. A shy man, a sound drinker, and utterly reliable.

ALICE C. COOPER, English head at Modesto, California, a gentle but reliable and scholarly lady of taste and originality.

EGBERT W. NIEMAN, of Shaker Heights, Ohio, English head, later junior high school principal, for a new incarnation of the seventh- and-eighth grade anthologies. After a year of work with Bert on *Adventures for Readers*, Book One, I tried to hire him as an inside editor but Bert didn't want to move his family to New York.

One of the great and permanent contributions to the *Adventures* series came from John Gehlman of Oak Park, Illinois, one of the origi- nal *Adventures* editors and Ernest Hemingway's high school English teacher: the inclusion of Thornton Wilder's *Our Town* as a major se- lection in *Adventures in American Literature*. This play has become a permanent part of the high school literature curriculum and nearly every eleventh-grade anthology has to have it in order to be compet- itive.

By this time the *Adventures* series had begun to burgeon. The first supplementary or alternate volume was *Adventures in World Litera- ture*, a fat 1350-page volume in the old favorite single column. It was edited by Rewey Belle Inglis, another of the original team and perhaps the most versatile and reliable *Adventures* editor of all, the Scotch Presbyterian, worthy English Head of the University High School of the University of Minnesota. Her collaborator was William K. Stew- art, my old favorite professor of Comparative Literature at Dartmouth. They made a splendid combination, with Rewey Belle's teaching know- how and Will Stewart's vast knowledge of world literature. *Adven- tures in World Literature* became a modest seller, but steady, so steady that it is still in print and going strong more than thirty years after first publication and only one token revision. Main reason for lack of drastic revision has always been cost: the original edition was set at cheap De- pression prices and today it would take at least three times the invest- ment to reset the book. But its modest sales helped Will Stewart's widow, Ethel, the marvelous hostess and good friend of undergradu- ates, who survived Will by some twenty years, to live into her high eighties gracefully and in some comfort in her Hanover house on Allen Street.

The other good anthology that budded from the main branch of the *Adventures* series was *Adventures in Modern Literature*, edited by a rare combination of talent and people: William C. Cunningham, the renegade Boston Irishman who was so delightful and full of just plain ability that he survived his escape from the Church—in Boston of all places!—and became one of the high school English heads. He was also one of the most naturally profane men I have ever known. Original and colorful profanity just flowed from him, in the corridors, the offices, or sometimes even in the classroom, but somehow coming from Bill in his absent-minded way it never seemed profane and nobody seriously objected. He was a remarkable writer and a lovely person! He introduced me to the Pilpel family of New York and Sandy Hook. It included the older sister, Mildred (Bill's wife), and the brilliant younger sister Harriet, who became a top copyright and book publishing lawyer in New York.

Bill's collaborator was the dignified, able Supervisor of English in Washington, D. C., Ruth Stauffer. They produced a fine book, of medium annual sales, that led eventually to a full-sized branch of the *Adventures* series especially for the less advantaged, or Track Two pupils,

In the forties we made two somewhat disappointing attempts to meet the needs of the disadvantaged students: (1) the *Discovery* series, a set of small topical collections started by Chester Persing, of Culver Military School and Bernice Leary, reading specialist of Madison, Wisconsin; and (2) the *Invitation to Reading* series, edited by my Providence, Rhode Island, friend Elmer Reid Smith. The one enduring small book to come out of this period was *Twenty Modern Americans*, by Alice Cooper of California, and Charles A. (Cap) Palmer, my old Dartmouth friend who had tried to lure me in 1928 from book publishing into his father's sewerpipe business. This business had failed in the Depression and Cap had pulled himself out by becoming a writer, first of stories and articles for magazines, then the one textbook that I snaggled him into, then of movie scripts and scenarios for Disney and other producers. Finally Cap started his own documentary film company, Parthenon Pictures, where he has won many awards and prizes. Cap has always kindly said that he needed my editorial blue pencil at the time of the writing of *Twenty Modern Americans* and that he benefited from the discipline of writing for a tough textbook editor. At any rate the outcome of the Cooper-Palmer collaboration and my editing was a little book that was a good seller and went unrevised for its twenty-five years of life. The table of contents shows the people we thought would interest high school pupils of the forties. Here is the list of short biographies of our twenty "modern" Americans:

WALT DISNEY, movie maker
THE MARTIN JOHNSONS, explorers
RICHARD EVELYN BIRD, pathfinder
AMELIA EARHART, aviatrix
WILLIAM BEEBE, naturalist
J. EDGAR HOOVER, G-man
HENRY AGARD WALLACE, public servant
GEORGE WASHINGTON CARVER, agricultural scientist
CHARLES PROTEUS STEINMETZ, electrical engineer
HELEN WILLS, tennis champion
YEHUDI MENUHIN, musician
MALVINA HOFFMAN, sculptress
THE MAYOS, doctors, surgeons
WILLIAM BUSHNELL STOUT, inventor
WALTER PERCY CHRYSLER, industrialist
PEARL S. BUCK, writer
WILLIAM ALLEN WHITE, journalist
WILL ROGERS, actor, writer
JANE ADDAMS, social worker
OLIVER WENDELL HOLMES, jurist

World War Two, I've always thought, rather snuffed out a social studies book we had great hopes for, *American Democracy Today and Tomorrow* by Helen F. Storen, Social Studies Supervisor of Hamtramck, Michigan, and Omar and Rhyllis Goslin, freelance researchers and writers. Helen brought the teaching knowhow and a productive steadiness to buttress Omar's somewhat wild creativeness and Rhyllis' writing ability. Omar knew a lot about visual appeal, layout, chart-making, and such things and their book I have always considered a real groundbreaker. Both Emerson Brown, by this time our full-time social studies editor, and I worked hard and faithfully on the Storen-Goslin book. It started out with a state adoption in Oregon but failed to catch on in other states or even in the open territories.

Our social studies list picked up momentum when Erling Hunt, after working with us on *America Organizes to Win the War*—and enjoying it—accepted our invitation to become our social studies editor. We paid him a yearly stipend and a general editor's royalty on books that came to us through him. Two highly successful textbooks came through Erling: *The World's History*, by two remarkable historians with Erling Hunt, and *America's History*, by the impressive collaboration of one of the great writers of American intellectual history and the editor of the magazine which served the social studies teachers association.

Frederic Lane, the quirky and difficult but highly talented economic historian of Johns Hopkins University, and Eric Goldman, never an "easy" author, but one of the best and most productive writers of historical prose in the profession, eventually full Professor of History at Princeton and "cultural" advisor to LBJ, collaborated with Erling Hunt on our world history for tenth graders. Lane's solid scholarship, Goldman's brilliant writing (he never wrote a dull paragraph), and Hunt's strategic position at Teachers College of Columbia University combined to produce a top textbook, though the three temperaments made an uneasy mixture which could, and did, loudly erupt from time to time. Lane was profoundly suspicious of everyone except Goldman; he never really believed we would actually publish the book; he resented all editing. Goldman was great fun as a social and drinking companion, but he came to have great scorn for Hunt, who was slow to deliver his part of the MS. Eric was always trying to get Hunt's share of the royalty reduced and this was difficult in view of Hunt's stiff New England parsimony. Emerson Brown and I wore pretty thin trying to keep this collaboration on the road, but we did it and the book came out in 1948 to become an important contender in tenth-grade world history adoptions, though it was never the top seller. Intellectually, it was a book we were proud of, for it represented a respectable solution of the difficult problem of condensing an account of seventy centuries of man's tortuous and myriad pathways on this earth to a year's course that a tenth-grade, fifteen-year-old American high school student of average ability had a fighting chance of understanding and appreciating! Goldman went on to become president of the American Historical Association, to be ringmaster of a famous TV program and advisor to LBJ.

The other prize that Erling brought to us was the collaboration of

Merle Curti, the gentle, vastly knowledgeable historical scholar of the University of Wisconsin, together with Paul Todd, versatile editor and professional writer and expositor. Paul not only had good stuff of his own and high school teaching experience, but also he could take Curti's material, give it the respect properly due it, and with deft re-write make it accessible to our audience of high school students. Curti went on to receive many prizes and to the presidency of the American Historical Association. Todd continued to edit *Social Education*, monthly organ of the social studies teachers' professional organization, and to contribute every week to *Civic Leader*, a weekly magazine for schools. *America's History* came out in 1948, had a modest success in this first edition, but had to wait the arrival in the fifties of Donald M. Stewart to edit its second edition and swiftly rise to the position of top best-selling senior high school American history. Finally, the authors—and Erling Hunt as general editor—made a potful!

The most frustrating failure of Emerson Brown and me in our work together was with Leon Marshall's extraordinary start toward a junior high school series of fused or integrated social studies books. Leon Marshall had been the head of the Economics Department at the University of Chicago until he quit to work on his MS. He had intellect powerful enough to bring together the various social sciences under the unifying umbrella of cultural anthropology—and the remarkable expository skill to make difficult concepts clear. The seventh-grade book, which we published in 1947, stands in my mind as a high-water mark in frontier thinking, good writing, careful and conscientious editing, and good bookmaking. But it didn't really go. It never received the all-out support of Dudley Meek or the sales staff. Also, it was an isolated book; it needed to be part of a series. But we were never able to find the right combination for the eighth- and ninth-grade books. And so we were never able to bring to fruition a competitor for Ginn's spectacular social studies series by Harold Rugg of Teachers College.

At one point, early in the effort for Marshall, I even had obtained the consent of James Michener, later the author of *South Pacific* and a dozen other sensationally selling books and movies, to collaborate with Marshall. At that time Michener was interested in leaving his teaching post at the State Teachers College in Greeley, Colorado. After reading Marshall's MS and a long session in our office, Jim Michener went down to Washington to spend the day with Marshall, came back to New York, and said he was willing to pitch in with him. But Leon Marshall turned Michener down! Then Michener went on to become Macmillan's social studies editor for a short while and eventually to the Pacific in World War Two and on into his fantastically successful writing career. And we were not able to get Marshall the collaborators he needed, so that Marshall's loner never got off the ground.

The good success in working with Erling Hunt spurred me to find and sign up general editors in other fields, both high school and college. Not in English, however, in either High School or College Department, for I felt no need for the supplementary knowledge and guidance or special contacts of a general editor. Perhaps the most valuable action was the signing of versatile and prolific Paul Brandwein, science head at Forest Hills High School in New York City, as our high school science editor—and prodigious author.

Dudley Meek and I got track of Paul first through his writing for educational magazines. It impressed us and in the spring of 1945 I sent Norman Hunter, our knowledgeable New York State man, out to Forest Hills to reconnoiter. Norman brought back a most enthusiastic report on Brandwein; I invited him in for a long lunch, and then signed him up. In *Exploring Biology* and *Your Health and Safety* we had a good science nucleus and with some speed Paul and I built our science list up, until in the sixties it was at the top, maybe Number One in the industry.

Paul Brandwein is one of those fabulous people who can and do work sixteen hours or more a day. That's how they find their happiness—in throwing their creative energy around! Paul knew a great many scientists and science teachers all over the country. He spoke and wrote constantly—all over the country. Soon we had signed up authors and collaborators for a three-book junior high school general science series, a physics text, a physical science text, and a chemistry. In addition, Paul was helping and advising me on revisions of *Exploring Biology* and *Your Health and Safety*. In coming to us Paul had put on ice his own partly completed biology MS (with a collaborator); he and Ella Thea Smith never did really hit it off. Paul was helpful in another way: when we needed to augment our inside staff of science editors,

Paul could usually come up with good suggestions. Throughout, Paul was generous and never narrowly self-serving. As a writer, his prolificity called for much intensive editing, which one way or another we were able to supply. Paul was sometimes edgy and temperamental but always together we solved each problem and/or crisis that came along.

In the College Department we made great progress in the forties, in part at least because of good new general editors. First to be signed up was J. Russell Whittaker, geography head at Peabody College of Education in Tennessee, and the darling of the geography profession. Russell himself was uncomfortable in his own writing, though his book, on conservation, is tops in a small field; but every geographer in this small, close-knit profession knew, liked, and trusted Russell. We had J. Russell Smith's brilliantly written *North America* from the twenties and Klim, Starkey, and Hall's *Economic Geography* from the thirties to build on and soon we had added a good basic text, *Introduction to Geography* by Henry M. Kendall, Robert M. Glendenning, and Clifford H. MacFadden, and Ralph Brown's historical geography (a small seller despite its getting all the business in its field). But after that we were stopped, for the class sizes in secondary and tertiary courses in geography were pretty small in the forties and fifties.

One of the most successful—and enduring—of the general editorships I founded was Ernest R. (Jack) Hilgard's in psychology. For years I had been trying but always defeated; I couldn't seem to get anywhere with the psychologists, though psychology was one of my trueloves. With one or two more psychology courses I could have had a major in it at Dartmouth. I found in my explorations and attempts to sign up authors that psychologists are more likely to get themselves tied in knots and fail to keep promises to produce MS than teachers in any other college discipline. But Jack Hilgard was different. Here was a man of science who kept his promises. He was head of the Psychology Department at Stanford and one of a particularly brilliant group of graduate students at Yale in the thirties. It was Gordon Allport, the wise, gentle psychologist of Harvard, who really put me on Hilgard's trail. I tracked him down in Washington, working during World War Two high up in the war effort there, and signed him as our general editor in psychology.

Even with Hilgard's mighty help, it was not easy to build the psychology list. We had two famous psychology books from the old International Library to start with: Kohler's *Mentality of Apes* and Koffka's *Growth of the Mind,* leaders in gestalt psychology. We were fortunate to get Lee Cronbach's *Educational Psychology,* which soon dominated its field for years and years. Cronbach, by 1950 a full Professor at the University of Illinois, was one of Terman's "geniuses," a group of young people of highest IQ whom Terman, the great intelligence test man, followed through the years. Cronbach was certainly one of the more successful ones. But Hilgard's own book, *Introduction to Psychology,* in its fourth edition in 1967 and selling nearly a quarter of a million copies annually, was and is the great book of the list.

Hilgard was a patient man, for he worked uncomplainingly with us in college editorial as we went all out to break the stranglehold of Scott Foresman's strong and attractive book, which overshadowed its competition in the large introductory psychology market. I started to edit Hilgard's MS sentence by sentence and paragraph by paragraph but found this fascinating but exacting intensive editing took more hours than the growing demands of my job would permit: so I had recourse to Percy Marks, that great editor and re-write man, and he worked with Hilgard for over a year. Later Hilgard said that Percy Marks "taught me to write" and that may in part be true. To meet—and if possible to beat—the strong visual appeal of the Scott Foresman book, I hired a special temporary art editor for the job. It turned out he was a wild man, who couldn't get along with other members of the staff. But he did have ideas, in tune with the coming revolution in textbook design, and helped us to make a smashing success of Hilgard's *Introduction to Psychology.* Jack went on to become president of the American Psychological Association, to continue his good experimental work, and to maintain his fine reputation for psychological *science.* Through the years I found Hilgard's judgments to be wise and sound, sound not only in psychology but in many human relations.

My greatly valued association with Robert K. Merton, who became our general editor in sociology, had a romantic start: I met him on the honeymoon of my second marriage. (The first marriage had broken up in 1943.) My bride Emmy, (who until a month before the wedding worked in the High School Department at HB) and I were in

Chapel Hill, home of the University of North Carolina, in April of 1945. We heard that Merton, a visiting professor from Columbia, was speaking at a seminar. We got permission to attend and were enormously impressed by him, acclaimed by every knowledgeable sociologist, as the coming young teacher and scholar. A short chat after the seminar led to a long lunch meeting when we were both back in New York. Known and liked throughout the profession, Merton was one of the most sparkling conversationalists I have ever known and, over the years, he became a valued friend. He himself found writing a bit slow, and so I never was able to get him to commit himself to write or collaborate on a beginning text. But soon we had some good men at work and the sociology list began to take shape: Wright Mills in social psychology, a wild creative genius who died too soon; William Kolb of Tulane; and magnetic Logan Wilson, also of Sophie Newcomb at Tulane. Wilson and Kolb collaborated on a new kind of book of readings in sociology: the selections knit together by long pieces of connective editorial commentary, which became a good success. Kroeber's *Anthropology* and the Lynd's *Middletown* and *Middletown in Transition* continued to sell steadily and well, so that the list altogether made a fine showing in the forties and fifties.

The going was harder in economics. After a brief and unfruitful period with Howard Ellis, the great money and banking man of the University of California at Berkeley, as our first general editor, my next move was highly successful: I signed up Paul Samuelson of MIT as our general editor, despite the fact that his own beginning textbook was being published by McGraw-Hill. Somehow I came late onto Samuelson; my spies didn't even tell me when his MS was up for bidding a year or two earlier. McGraw-Hill got it and it became one of the biggest selling—and one of the best—textbooks of the century. We had by this time signed up Arthur Burns, Alfred Neal, and Donald Watson, of George Washington University, for a "new kind" of beginning economics textbook. We worked hard on it and brought it out the same spring as Samuelson; it had a fine sale the first year or two, but lost out to Samuelson in the long pull. Both books helped to revolutionize the teaching of economics by introducing the national income approach, a post-Keynesian kind of economics which rather rapidly replaced the outworn "principles" approach.

Paul Samuelson, McGraw-Hill author, and Paul Samuelson, general editor for HB, made an uneasy mixture and soon Paul asked to be released. He did, however, lead me to Albert Gaylord Hart, the brilliant, rapid-fire economist of Columbia. Albert and I worked happily together, building an economics list. Albert was himself a good writer and the author of a successful book on money and banking for Prentice-Hall, but he had at once the worst handwriting I have ever seen and his thoughts constantly outran his capacity for oral output. We had of course the prestige of being Keynes' publisher, the moderate success of Horace Taylor's *Contemporary Economic Problems*, as well as a fine book in labor economics, *Unions, Management, and the Public*, by Wight Bakke of Yale and Clark Kerr of the University of California, to build on. Soon we added an *American Economic History* by Ross Roberston, and eventually an introductory text by Paul Homans, the longtime secretary of the American Economic Association and Professor at UCLA and Albert Hart himself. But somehow the going in economics was never as good as it should have been.

In my personal and publishing life there have been five college presidents: [1] W. H. Cowley of Hamilton College, Harlan Hatcher of the University of Michigan, Logan Wilson of the University of Texas, Clark Kerr of the University of California, and Benjamin Wright, Jr. of Smith College.

Cowley, my roommate of sophomore year at Dartmouth, as I have said, always seemed destined to be a college president and he was, except for a lack of tact, well-equipped for the job. After obtaining his Ph.D. at the University of Chicago, Hal taught at Ohio State for several years and finally got the bid for the presidency of Hamilton College in upper New York State. Here, as expected by all who knew him, Hal conducted a revolution, which over the years alienated much of the faculty and led finally to his withdrawal. At one

[1] *Toward the end of 1968, after the section on my five college presidents had been written, my friend and author S. I. Hayakawa was made acting president of San Francisco State College. Since then he has had a rough but not unhappy (for I know how realistic and tough Hayakawa is) time battling the extremists on that roiling and broiling campus. I do not think he will be tinged with "guilt by association" with Ronald Reagan, though some of his erstwhile friends and admirers have jumped to wrong conclusions.*

point, Hal was offered the job of president of the University of Minnesota, a larger job at a larger place with which, paradoxically I think, he might have had better total success. But in good conscience, Hal turned Minnesota down because he had started so many things he felt "he had to see through at Hamilton." A great mistake, in my view. Hal has ended up as a tall, greying, handsome Professor of Higher Education at Stanford, where he has trained, he says, twenty college presidents, and many other college administrators.

I got to know Harlan Hatcher when he was a professor of English at Ohio State, a tall, greying, handsome man. We worked together on a big collection of modern world drama, which HB published in several packages: a huge complete book, with thirty-one plays, which in turn we broke into three volumes: a volume of eight American plays, one of seven English plays, and one of sixteen Continental plays—all with introductions and comments by Harlan Hatcher. HB paid the sizable permission costs, and what seemed at the time a handsome fee to Hatcher. I have since thought it would have been better and fairer to have given him a royalty. But cash money in the Depression years and even into the forties was often most welcome to a college professor. At any rate, Harlan did a great job in play selection, editing, and introducing; his books, in their various incarnations have sold well, especially the Shorter Edition which we published later. It was a pleasure working with him; never a serious argument or dispute. He had a knack for getting along with people, a quality which must have smoothed over many a difficult situation in his big job as president of the University of Michigan. It also helps if a college president is tall, handsome, and articulate as Harlan emphatically was on all three counts.

Like Hatcher, Logan Wilson was tall, greying into a striking handsomeness, and articulate. He came to HB through Robert K. Merton, and he was a good writer, hard worker, and good friend, with an eye for the ladies as they had an eye for him. He also was as liberal a Southerner as I have known. Soon after publication of *Sociological Analysis* by Wilson and Kolb, Logan became vice-president of the University of North Carolina and not long after the president of the University of Texas. Both jobs he filled with distinction and at last reports he was head of the American Council on Education in Washington, D.C.

Unlike my other four college presidents, Clark Kerr, the most brilliant of them all, was not tall, or grey, or particularly handsome. He was a discovery of John McCallum's, who ran across him in the early forties as a Professor of Labor Economics at the University of California in Berkeley. There Clark Kerr not only taught wisely and well, but he made frequent forays out into the jungle of labor disputes as a negotiator and arbitrator—an extraordinarily successful one. He had a Quaker background and a reserved quietness, but when a decision was called for he could leap into action like a tiger, talk with the greatest persuasiveness, and swing a meeting or conference with spectacular effectiveness. Few of Clark Kerr's great qualities were readily apparent in his relationships at HB; but they were there under the surface. John and I persuaded him to collaborate with Wight Bakke of Yale on a big book of readings, *Labor, Management, and the Public*, with the readings so cemented together by Bakke and Kerr's commentary that the total effect was that of a good solid textbook. It always was a highly respected book and sold with steady moderation. Clark Kerr became Chancellor of the Berkeley branch of the U of C and finally overall president of the whole California university system, where he fought the good fight with great success. However, in the early sixties, reactionary Governor Ronald Reagan and his reactionary allies on the Board of Regents, finally outnumbered Kerr and ousted him. A disgraceful performance by a slick, lightweight political climber! For Clark Kerr, in my book, is a truly great man. His brilliant recent books on higher education are better written than anything he wrote for us. I can't claim that we taught him, either. He grew on the job at Berkeley, big as he and it were.

My fifth college president was Benjamin Wright, Jr., tall, not too handsome, and red-headed. He was our general editor in political science for several years, when he was Professor of Government at Harvard before becoming President of Smith College, the great woman's college at Northampton, Massachusetts, known as "Hamp" to all Dartmouth men. Over the years, our relationship can best be described as "red-headed." Ben and I worked hard, talked to and got many good men almost to the point of commitment, but never quite got enough commitments to build a top list. Two really good books came out of the Ben Wright general editorship: *Major Foreign Powers* by Gwendolyn Carter and John Ranney, still the finest book in comparative government, now many times revised and always a good seller. Ranney died much too soon, but Gwen Carter, a gallant woman, carried on. Harold Stein's *Cases in Public Administration*, a high quality book that never sold very well, was the other. None of Ben Wright's successors did very well either. We tried but never could pin down Pendleton Herring, top man in public administration.

In neither English nor history did we in College Editorial feel the need for a general editor. In both fields we were strong—and continued strong. It was in the early forties that we published the first edition of John Hodges' *The Harbrace Handbook*, HB's college bestseller of all time. John Hodges was "discovered" and pushed by Sydney Stanley, and others of our salesmen who called on him. For at least ten years Hodges, in charge of freshman English at the University of Tennessee, had kept in his archives all the themes the Tennessee freshmen wrote—and what's more he had analyzed them to discover the most frequent types of errors. He substituted precise research for the usual "informed guess" based on teaching experience. Thus armed he set about writing a handbook of English to compete with Wooley's *Handbook of English* (D. C. Heath & Co.) and *The Century Handbook* (Appleton-Century-Crofts), which together occupied much of the biggest of all college markets, the freshman English course. We signed Hodges up; I worked with Bob Josephy and Howard Clark on a drastic new design in which the rules appeared in the boldest of bold black type; and John McCallum did a great job of editing. In the quarter century since its appearance, Hodges' *Harbrace Handbook*, now with collaborators and successors and many revisions, clearly leads this big field and sells over a quarter of a million copies annually! John Hodges was always a pleasure to work with, a fine Southern craftsman and gentleman. He taught me to drink the "Black Velvet," a subtle combination of champagne and Guiness' stout, a sure preventive of seasickness.

It was just after the end of World War Two that we signed up Robert Penn Warren and Cleanth Brooks for the great book that became *Modern Rhetoric*. Never the great seller that *Understanding Poetry* (Holt) was this prestigious book sold well and gave me the wonderful experience of working closely with two of the most creative college teachers of our times. Soon after the Brooks-Warren contract was signed, the young editor who mediated the deal decided he wanted trade rather than text publishing and resigned.

But soon this loss was more than made up when I hired a new editor, William I. Jovanovich, who eventually became president of HB. It was late summer of 1946 when my wife Emmy and I were visiting Howard and Bess Jones, up from Harvard, at their summer place in Peachum, Vermont. We had driven down from our vacation spot at Island Pond, Vermont, for a swim, steak over the outdoor fireplace, and overnight with the Joneses, by now our good friends. I asked Howard if he had any graduate students lying around loose who might make good textbook editors. Howard thought a moment and said yes, there was one good possibility: Bill Jovanovich, fresh out of the Navy, was taking graduate work at Columbia and trying to make a living for himself, wife, and baby by copyediting.

It was early October before I made contact with Jovanovich. He came down to the office at 383 Madison Avenue for an interview. I hadn't talked to him more than five minutes before I was trying to hire him. He was from Denver, fifteen years behind my time there, the son of a labor leader from Montenegro. He'd gone to Manual Training High School, instead of East Denver High School as I had, then to the University of Colorado, majoring in literature, and playing a little basketball, for he was a great tall young man, finally to Harvard for graduate study in American literature under Howard Mumford Jones, which was interrupted by Pearl Harbor. He served as an officer in charge of stores in the Navy, met and married a beautiful girl, Martha, the belle of Mobile, during his service, and now was just ripe, I thought, for a career in book publishing. But Bill Jovanovich turned me down, as I had explained that we expected our editors to do some traveling and selling. Bill said he didn't want to leave his family alone that long. Later, I understood why, as they had a walk-up apartment in the Lower Bronx, near Morris High School. However, I found myself unwilling to accept this decision and returned to the charge in January, 1947, making the concession that Bill would not have to travel out of the city. Bill finally said he would take the job and before the spring was over, he himself was asking to travel, to have a sales territory. He had come to see the sense of it. In recent years he has even gone so far as to claim that he was hired as a salesman, but this is not true. I hired him as an editor and he worked exclusively as an editor in the office his first three months with HB.

The second half of the decade of the forties and well into the fifties I was fortunate in having what must have been the most high-powered staff of textbook editors in the industry. Here is my all-star cast that was:

The President of Harcourt, Brace & World (Bill Jovanovich)
The Executive Vice-President of Harcourt, Brace & World for many
   years (John H. McCallum)
The Chairman of the Board of Macmillan (Lee C. Deighton)
A Vice-President of McGraw-Hill (Emerson Brown)

What a group to work with! I must say that we turned out a lot of work and together laid the basis for the remarkable expansion of the Textbook Department in the fifties. Lee Deighton, who had been brought on from the managership of the Chicago office in 1945, spent only about half of his time editing, mostly English books but some social studies and science, too. The other half he functioned as general sales manager of the High School Department. I've always thought he was a better editor than sales manager. He delighted, as he used to say, "in running a MS through my typewriter." When he did, the MS came out a lot sharper, clearer, and better than it went in. At Dudley Meek's urging, Deighton was soon made a director. Emerson Brown was in full swing, doing his best work on *The World's History, America's History*, and launching the first of our highly successful "state" books, *Exploring New York State*. John McCallum was doing the work of two or three editors in the College Department, and WIJ (he dropped the middle "I" in the middle fifties) began his tremendous work and growth. With all these fine and able people working for and with me, I felt I had indeed arrived "on the uplands."

In all this I had the steady backing of SSS and until about 1948 the willing cooperation of Dudley Meek. After the Harcourts departed and he became president, Don Brace was less remote. Don exerted his leadership but gently. One day, for example, most of us directors were at lunch at the Oak Room, downstairs at the Ritz Carlton right across Madison Avenue from the office. All the directors except AH were there, though it was not in any sense a formal meeting. Don led off the discussion and great arguments followed, winding up precisely where Don's original analysis had put us. Don quietly remarked, "I should throw my weight around more!" Perhaps he should have, but it was not in his nature. His desk at the office piled higher and higher and sss took on more company-wide responsibilities, leaving more of the pure textbook decisions and motive power to Dudley Meek and me. Soon sss's increased role was recognized by the Board of Directors, which made him general manager as well as vice-president. Shortly after the Harcourts left in 1942, Dudley Meek, on Frank Morley's nomination as I remember it, took Hastings' place as secretary of the Company. Thus DM got a leg up in our under-the-surface power struggle. I think my position had been weakened about 1937 when both DM and I had an opportunity to buy some more common stock. At the time I thought I had the choice of building a fine new home in Stamford (my wife Helen Grace Carlisle had sold a book to the movies) or of putting money into HB. Now this was clearly the wrong decision, for the marriage foundered a few years later and the house stayed in my possession only a few years, whereas the stock went on to multiply in value many times over. Furthermore, the decision seemed to suggest that I wanted to be less deeply involved in the Company than DM did. Too bad!

The Trade Department was a lively operation under Don Brace and Frank Morley, and, under them, Robert Giroux and, for a few years, Stanley Young, who wanted to have a play produced on Broadway even more than he wanted to publish good trade books. These were the years when Saroyan was in fullest bloom, despite an editorial trick that Frank Morley played on him. Saroyan had written *The Human Comedy* in Hollywood as a script for the movies, and Frank was after him, without much success, to expand it to a long story or novel. Finally, Saroyan agreed to let another writer make the adaptation. Frank deliberately chose a third-rater, for he knew that when Saroyan read the MS this writer produced he would be so angry that he would turn to and do the job himself. Well, it worked precisely as planned. As mentioned earlier, Frank had some other good writers on his lists; and some of the old reliables like Carl Sandburg and Dorothy Canfield were of course producing. But Frank viewed the rise of sss and the threatened return of AH with increasing alarm, and finally decided to return to London and his own writing.

Frank Morley's departure left the door wide open for the acquisition of Reynal & Hitchcock, one of Don Brace's best strokes. Eugene Reynal had been the bright young man picked by HB and three other publishers to run Blue Ribbon Books, a reprint house set up in 1930 by the four publishers to handle their reprints. Gene Reynal had made a good success of it and, in 1933, used some of his independent wealth to purchase Blue Ribbon and then set up his own publishing company in partnership with another good young man, perhaps even more talented than Reynal, Curtice Hitchcock of Appleton-Century. The new company did well, especially with Lillian Smith's *Strange Fruit*, one of the great novels of the thirties. They also had St. Exupéry, the great French writer (*The Little Prince* and *Wind, Sand, and Stars*) and P. L. Travers (*Mary Poppins*) on their list. Curtice Hitchcock died during World War Two and the company never quite recovered from this loss, so that it was available to Don Brace's offer in 1946. Gene Reynal came to HB as a director and head of the Trade Department and for many years made a good showing. Reynal also brought with him Ed Hodge, a great trade sales manager, who by himself made the acquisition of Reynal & Hitchcock worthwhile. Reynal had the wisdom to permit Robert Giroux to develop rapidly as a top trade editor.

It was in 1948, six years after the fracas over Hastings and the Harcourt's departure for California, that Alfred Harcourt returned and took control again of the Company. We younger directors (Dudley Meek, Gene Reynal, Lee Deighton, and I) had been uneasy but somehow we were not surprised that he was taking charge. Don Brace knew that the stockholders' "iron triangle" had worked once more: sss had switched to the Harcourts. In the reorganization, Don was retired as president and sss became the new president, DM became treasurer, and Reynal a vice-president. AH spitefully insisted that we break relations with Melville Cane (the Company's long-term lawyer) whom he made a sort of scapegoat for siding with Don. I was about to be left as a plain director, when Lee Deighton did me a great turn: he urged me to go to AH and assure him that I had long ago severed all connections with the Book and Magazine Guild, and other "leftist" connections, and would like to be secretary of the Company. Without further ado, AH agreed, sss agreed, and I became an officer of HB. AH didn't spend much time in New York or at the office, and Hastings stayed in California for the most part. After a brief interlude Don Brace decided to come in pretty much as usual. sss pitched into his new job as president, but we all knew where the power was.

CHAPTER SEVEN
GROWTH
AND STRUGGLES
(1948-1953)

THE COLD WAR BEGAN ROUGHLY IN 1948—in the world and at HB. Altogether this six-year span was the roughest and hardest in my whole time at HB, particularly its last half, which coincided with the Joseph McCarthy era in the nation and the Korean War in the world.

It all began innocently enough. Truman won his re-election, much to most people's surprise, but to my delight, for I greatly admired Truman. He had the intelligence and courage to make three of the toughest decisions a human being was ever called on to make: to drop the atom bomb and end the war against Japan; to decide almost instantly whether to fight a just and honorable war in Korea to save the UN and to stop Stalin and the Communists; and to fire the romantic and popular MacArthur, thus reasserting civilian rule over the military. I can remember being bewitched, at this time, by Eisenhower and hoping that he would run as a Democrat. But I worked and voted for Truman in 1948, as I had for Roosevelt in 1944, traveling with poet Bill Benét, and the great teacher and poet, Mark Van Doren, with a sound truck and making speeches on street corners. Bill Jovanovich voted for Henry Wallace on the third party ticket though I had tried to talk Bill out of it.

Business at HB was flourishing, notably in the College Department. It benefited from the influx of GI's into the colleges, beginning in 1946 but reaching large proportions in the years 1948-1950. It was not only that college enrollments were strikingly up, but the GI's had money to spend on their education, including textbooks. Furthermore, the veterans of World War Two were older, often married, and altogether more serious about education than the traditional college boys. Joe College pretty much disappeared from the campuses and the mature, serious returned veteran dominated the halls of learning. College teachers loved this and quickly lifted their sights—and their requirements. College education took a giant leap forward in the GI period.

HB benefited in another way from the return of the World War Two veterans. We recruited some of the best talent in the history of the company: WIJ, for one; Cameron Moseley, who eventually came to head the High School Department; Mel Means, state adoption expert and for some years later on the manager of the Chicago office; Paul Corbett, who came to us from Canada via the University of Chicago Press, eventually to head the College Department; Kermit Patton, who succeeded Howard Clark after his death as head of production; ex-fighter pilot Dick Tietjen; Jack Gallagher (a great "close" editor); Jim Milholland who eventually got the Company into the farm newspaper business; and many others.

About this time the malaise of male middle age—restlessness—hit both Dudley Meek and me. His restlessness took the form of his interest going outside the strict textbook business to investigate educational films. He and William Spaulding, of Houghton Mifflin, both active in the American Textbook Publishers Institute (ATPI), spent much time outside of the office heading an investigation of the possibilities of hooking up films to textbooks in some way, or in discovering whether textbook publishers had a special contribution to make to educational films. After a couple of years of flirtation with movies, they decided the time was not ripe and relationship was not likely to be fruitful. Actually down to this writing, McGraw-Hill has been the only publisher to make a major effort in films, and they have built it up over the years into a large and profitable part of their business.

Dudley took congenially to his new responsibility as treaurer of HB. He found the able William W. Vickery, and placed him over Hettie Wilson as comptroller and head of accounting. Together DM and Vickery put in new systems and new machines just in time for our big expansion of the fifties and sixties. Also DM led the way at ATPI in setting up uniform accounting practices so that the annual Industry Report on sales, costs, prices, and all the key business figures became an instrument of great value to managers. No one company could be identified in these but a company could insert its own figures and see how they compared to industry averages and spreads. A major and permanent contribution!

My restlessness took the form of exploring the possibility of starting a magazine, *New Perspectives*, we called it, with two of my friends: Peter Cary, of *Reader's Digest*, and Theodore M. Ferro, a freelance writer. It was fun talking and exploring, but Carl Sandburg finally put an end to our dreamy little effort when he said he'd not collaborate or even contribute. He wisely said, "Stick to the textbooks, which you're really good at."

It was toward the end of World War Two that an old Denver association of mine came to life and led to the publication of probably the most important book of my career. I was at work at my old desk in the bullpen shared with sss and Marian Abernethy when the receptionist called and said there was a Dr. Roe from the Yale School of Alcohol Studies to see me. As I entered the reception room this tall, good-looking woman of about my own age rose, looked at me, and said, "Why, aren't you Jimmie Reid of East Denver High School?" I admitted it and then she explained that she was Anne Roe, now a clinical psychologist at Yale, my old high school classmate and friend and political supporter. We hadn't seen each other since high school but it turned out when I took her to lunch that she had married George Gaylord Simpson, whom I had known since our days as ten-year-olds at the Denver YMCA. At the moment George was on Eisenhower's staff in the Italian campaign. I learned from Anne that George had become one of the world's leading research scientists, strong in both biology and geology. No surprise, as George and I were the same age, but he was so bright and fast that he had sped through high school years ahead of me and had gone to the University of Colorado and then on to Yale to get his Ph.D. in geology.

In addition to her own research at Yale, Anne was looking after George's daughters from his first (eventually tragic and unhappy) marriage. She would look me up when she came to New York and let me take her to lunch or dinner and when the war was over George returned to the American Museum of Natural History uptown in New York and became head of vertebrate paleontology there. I had been divorced and remarried by that time and the Simpsons and the Reids began to see a good deal of each other out of office hours.

We founded "The Mandolin and Whiskey Club," with six members: two Simpsons, two Reids, Dr. Harold Harris (a leading authority on brucellosis, a wonderfully unorthodox doctor), and his attractive nurse, Blanche Stevenson. Our meetings were likely to be irregular since Harold and Blanche split their medical time between practices in upstate Westport on Lake Champlain and New York City, nearly 400 miles apart. But we would meet as often as possible for an evening at one or another's apartment for drinks, talk, and dinner. Then to the music. George and I played conventional, old-fashioned mandolins, and Harold a somewhat louder banjo-mandolin. Anne was anchor-woman, first at her guitar and then when her fingers began to wear down she'd shift to the piano and with either instrument strive to hold us three bull-mandoliners together. My wife Emmy and Blanche saw to it that the musicians did not run dry. Mostly we played from Carl Sandburg's *The American Songbag* (the great HB book) and *The Fireside Book of Folksongs*, (also great, from Simon and Schuster). We had many favorites, including "Red River Valley" and "The Erie Canal," but our theme song or national anthem was "Hatikvah," the legendary song of the Jewish migration to Israel. We always ended up our evenings with that. The Mandolin and Whiskey Club met for well over ten years; it was finally broken up when Harold and Blanche terminated the New York City end of the practice and the Simpsons received appointments to Harvard. George became Alexander Agassiz Professor of Vertebrate Paleontology and Anne (a bit later) the first woman full professor in the Harvard Graduate School of Education. And George and Anne were the first Harvard full professors married to each other!

For several of the years of the late forties I had been trying to interest George in writing a college textbook in general biology. For this, he was superbly equipped: he had a range of firm knowledge equalled only by Julian Huxley and one or two other biologists in the world. Furthermore, he could *write*—precisely, clearly, and eloquently. His teaching was minor, mostly to graduate students, but he could write to an audience and with some help from collaborators and the experienced editing I knew we at HB could supply, the skimpy teaching background was not important.

In the summer of 1950 the Simpsons invited the Reids, including Jamie, 15, to vacation at Los Pinavetes, their ranch, 8000 feet above sea level, and the last habitation before a national forest took over the rest of the big mountain in northern New Mexico. What a view, a hundred miles across the desert to the Chuska range on the Arizona border! This was the month the Korean War started and while we followed it, fascinated, we were too deep in the scenic and scientific wonders of that magnificent western landscape to be really worried. Jamie and I accompanied George, scrambling around the dry desert hills, on a few of his fossil-hunting expeditions but of course lacked the educated eye to be of real help in spotting outcroppings of old bones. But one day, on an overnight expedition, which I missed, George made a discovery of considerable size and importance to science and the American Museum. In an arroyo, a considerable drive from home base, he ran across some fossil bones, well-preserved, which George figured out to be the bones of a prehistoric beast called *Coryphodon*. It turned out to be a rich deposit. Catching George at the height of his elation over the *Coryphodon*, I put the final proposal for the college biology to him and to my great joy and excitement he said "*Yes,*" and one of the truly great textbooks of the twentieth century was at last on its way!

In 1956 trouble struck George Gaylord Simpson. By that time most of the work was done on the MS for *Life*, his college biology text. He organized and headed a party for the American Museum to search a tributary of the Amazon River for possible beds of fossils. His party had pressed far up the Jurua River to the southwest, had achieved its objectives, and was now headed back to civilization.

Making bivouac one evening on the shore of the river, a Brazilian man was helping clear away jungle on a twenty-foot cliff above the river. He forgot to call "Timber!" in time. The falling tree caught George and smashed both legs, the right one most severely. When he came back to consciousnss, he supervised what first-aid was available and the preparation of a stretcher to carry him down the cliff to a houseboat waiting in the river.

They started in all good speed for the nearest riverport, on the Jurua

River. George estimated they were fifteen hours away, when the first of several good breaks occurred. An Indian in a fast canoe came alongside and an exchange was made, so that the running time to the riverport was considerably reduced. By this time George was in great pain and his wounded legs were getting worse.

At the riverport another fortunate break occurred. A bushpilot in his amphibian flew into the primitive airport and the pilot flew George to Manaus on the Amazon, where there was a doctor and a hospital of sorts. Here came another bit of good luck. The Brazilian doctor administered what George described as "second aid," and realized that there was no surgeon or hospital short of the States who could do right by George's very bad legs. And so the Brazilian doctor of Manaus came right along to attend George on both the flight to Belém at the Amazon's mouth and on the long flight to New York. Here was another good break: the Pan American plane which flew George to New York was one of the few at that time with a bed, so George could lie down.

As the plane approached Idlewild (now Kennedy) Airport, Anne had a surgeon of the University Hospital in Manhattan waiting at the hospital, and an ambulance on its way to Idlewild. Then an impossible fog descended, and both Idlewild and LaGuardia were shut down, leaving Newark the only metropolitan possibility. George's plane just made it there before the fog clamped down, but he had to sit for an hour and a half in the Newark Airport while the ambulance made its slow way through traffic to pick him up.

Once arrived at University Hospital, the surgeons put George to bed for build-up and a couple of days of rest before the necessary long and difficult surgery on his legs. It was years before George recovered and even today he is a bit gimpy. It happened that both George and I were on canes one day in the late fifties (I had the hip operation in 1955), when George came to lunch. As we struggled through the revolving door of the office building, George said wryly, "We look like the Decoration Day parade!"

Publishing a really great textbook, such as Simpson's *Life* or Brooks and Warren's *Understanding Poetry* (Holt, 1938), is like tossing a stone into a mill pond.[1] The ripples spread and spread and reach many

---

[1] *This metaphor is taken—without permission—from one of John Ciardi's essays.*

shores. In the first place, *Life* stepped up the intellectual level of the beginning college course in biology just at the time when everyone, consciously or subconsciously, was seeking it. Even junior colleges, which in all rationality perhaps should not have tried to emulate the top colleges by using the same teaching materials, adopted *Life*, a pretty tough book. Its use became really widespread. In the second place, its influence spread even to the high school course in biology through "The Biological Science Curricular Study," which, starting in the late fifties, after Sputnik, revolutionized the secondary school course. In the third place, the good royalties brought greater financial security. Finally, the impact of *Life* has been memorialized, unintentionally of course, by the competitors; many of them are frankly imitative and others say they do the same job only easier. George Simpson had collaborators, several of them, he says, very good, but *Life* is *his* book.

In the middle and late forties two greatly talented and powerful high school teachers of grammar and language came to add their strength to our high school list: John Warriner, head of the English Department of the Garden City, Long Island, High School and Joseph Blumenthal, head of the English Department of the MacKenzie High School, Detroit. Separately and together as collaborators, they produced big-selling and long-term selling books for HB.

In the fall of '45 Ned Bradford, salesman and promotion manager at the time and later a vice-president of Little Brown, came in and said he'd found a good man named John Warriner with the MS, practically complete, for a high school handbook of English. So I telephoned Warriner and asked him and his MS in for lunch. One can't help but like John instantly. He is tall and awkward, with a touch of the legendary Ichabod Crane, but what he says always makes sense. A quick reading of his MS revealed its superior quality. Not only were John's explanations of the intricacies of English grammer clear and sensible but his supporting drills and practice materials were extraordinarily lively and interesting instead of dry and dead. He obviously knew high school kids and how to appeal to their interests without in any way cheapening the appeal. Furthermore, he made great sense in avoiding "motivation" on the composition or creative side of language teaching. John always said that the teacher in the classroom, taking advantage of day-to-day and local happenings, could do a better job of motivating themes than any textbook. And so he stuck to the technical and organizational side of the teaching of writing. Most teachers, including usually the department heads and other good ones, agreed with this no-nonsense approach.

John was easy to work with, never touchy or irritable. He even could make deadlines, with able help in preparing the MS from his hard-working and lively wife, Dotty. Soon Warriner's *Handbook of English*, aimed mainly at grades nine and ten, appeared and immediately began to sell well. There developed a demand for a Warriner handbook for grades eleven and twelve, and we set to work with John to produce it, thus giving the salesmen a modest series. Warriner's *Handbook of English: Book Two* soon was selling well, too, and John was on his way to unsuspected affluence.

Joe Blumenthal, on the other hand, was not an "easy" author to work with; he was sensitive and sometimes moody, but in his entirely different way he was as fine a teacher and writer as John Warriner. Joe Blumenthal always said he had developed over about twenty years one small specialty: "the teaching of grammar to high school students." Joe's pupils mainly were in the disadvantaged districts of Detroit, unlike John's more affluent suburban pupils. It was Lee Deighton who "discovered" Joe, but I had the fun of working with him on his first project: a series of two workbooks, *Common Sense English*, primarily for pupils who were discouraged with, or allergic to, traditional grammar. Joe had invented a system for teaching grammar with a whole fresh and easy-to-remember set of labels. For example, a verb was an "action word," and a pronoun was a "substitute word," and so on. In addition Joe had a great gift for patient and clear explanation, and, like John Warriner, a knack for producing drill materials interesting and to the point. The *Common Sense English* books sold but modestly; however, they built up such a loyal following that, unrevised, twenty years later they are still in print and still selling. Blumenthal's break with the traditional grammar labels was more than most teachers could take and this severely limited the sales appeal. Nevertheless, our confidence in Joe Blumenthal never wavered and presently Lee Deighton came up with an idea for a series of workbooks on which Warriner and Blumenthal could collaborate.

The English Workshop series consisted of workbooks for the four high school years, two by Warriner and two by Blumenthal, and edited in our shop by Deighton. They became big sellers immediately and with timely revisions and expansion into the seventh and eighth grades have lasted many years. Traditional grammar, yes, but with sparkle and sense.

Then Blumenthal got switched into the *Living Language* series, a series sensitive and responsive to new developments in language research, advanced thinking and teaching about language. The series took a long time going through the works at HB, partly because Deighton was splitting his energies between sales supervision and editing and finally left the Company. Upon publication the series was esteemed highly but sold modestly, never in the big figures that Joe Blumenthal had envisaged.

John Warriner became involved in a gigantic expansion of his two handbooks into a six-book series for the junior and senior high school years. The idea for the expanded series evolved in an informal talk session in the late hours one September after all-day sessions at sales meetings at the Absecon Country Club near Atlantic City. Top executives, editors, and sales managers of HB's High School Department were talking and helping to shape up the idea of a series of six Warriner handbooks. We all contributed and the excitement and appeal of the plan grew on us all. Upon returning to the office the next Monday, I started full force to gain John Warriner's cooperation, which was easy, for John was eager and willing, and to set up the right collaborators for him. To prepare and publish a six-book series all in the space of three years was a staggering assignment, even though we had the model and some of the material in the two existing Warriner handbooks. So I got busy on long distance in a bull-like rush.

John himself would do the entire twelfth-grade book and be the major author on the tenth grade one. His main collaborator on the eleventh-grade book was Joseph Mersand, head of a New York City English department. For the main work on the ninth-grade book and to assist John on the tenth-grade book, I had the inspiration to pick Mary Whitten, who had "helped" John Hodges at the University of

Tennessee on a revision of *The Harbrace Handbook*. Mary, it turned out, had shifted to a teachers college in Denton, Texas, and when I telephoned, was out fishing in the Gulf of Mexico. But when she came home, she found King Burney, our Texas man, sitting on her doorstep. For the seventh- and eighth-grade books, which were the hardest since they had to be done from scratch, I signed up John Treanor, principal of a Boston Intermediate School, and George Shaftel, a sparky free-lance writer. These lower two books and the eleventh-grade book gave us the most trouble and probably we wouldn't have made it anywhere near on schedule without the titan help of Bill Frankel, refugee from the *Random House Dictionary* and free-lance writer extraordinary! But we did make it and the Warriner series came out to end the Tressler monopoly of D. C. Heath's, to beat other competition, and to sell its fantastic millions of copies. Success did not spoil John Warriner. He finally felt it was safe to retire from his $10,000-a-year teaching job and live on his fat, well-gotten gains.

Another rewarding experience in the fifties was working with Frank Jennings (later a roving editor for the *Saturday Review*) and Charles Calitri (later a successful novelist) on a most original collection of short stories, still a good steady seller.

After founding and then personally editing the *Adventures* series for twenty years, I decided it would be a good thing for the series and its future not only to continue the flow of fresh talent into the authorship but this time to switch the chief inside editor. And the proper replacement was at hand in the person of the new brilliant rising star, Bill Jovanovich. In his first few years as a working editor he had performed beautifully each assignment and, with a fair segment of his time now devoted to selling, he was as ready for the big opportunity as the series was ready for a new editor.

First, to give Bill the feel of the work and to try him out, I asked him to edit the revision of *Adventures in Modern Literature*. He did a good job. Each editor has his own style, and Bill's was more heavy-handed than mine. He himself is a good writer and his tendency was to re-write the introductions and other material handed in by the *Adventures* authors; whereas I tended to reshape, clean up, and tighten, leaving the essential flavor of the original writer. Having seen in his work on *Adventures in Modern Literature* that Bill was really good—as well as different—I gave him the big job of editing the 1952 revision of the four main *Adventures* anthologies. Not only that, but also the almost overwhelming task of getting all four out together in time for certain state adoptions. Before the '52 edition we had usually staggered publication dates over two or three years. Bill took on this gigantic editing job, and though I offered to buttress him with additional editorial help, he preferred to do the whole Herculean task himself. Also, the seventh- and eighth-grade *Adventures* volumes were to follow in 1953 and an adaptation of the top four anthologies, the Cardinal Newman Edition for Catholic Schools, was to come along in 1954—all under his aegis. We had developed great plans for expansion and we were ready to meet the stringent requests of the salesmen for simultaneous series publication, a great sales advantage. Houghton Mifflin, under their fine but deliberate editor Norris Hoyt, never did catch on to the great advantage we gained and continued the old plodding staggered publication of their series. Other publishers were also slow to catch on.

Bill had some fine new talent in the authorship I had gathered for him to work with: Evan Lodge, minor poet and director of English in Cleveland, Ohio, who came in to help marvelous old Blanche Jennings Thompson and Jack Ross on *Adventures in Reading*, the ninth-grade book; Susanna Baxter of Galveston, the only King Burney nominee to give less than promised, working with that fine pair of veterans, Luella B. Cook of Minneapolis, and Walter Loban, now Professor of the Teaching of English at the University of California at Berkeley, on *Adventures in Appreciation;* John Gehlman still at Oak Park, Illinois (Ernest Hemingway's old high school); Wilbur Schramm, now head of the University of Illinois Press; sure-fire Mary Bowman of Texas on *Adventures in American Literature;* and Donald A. Stauffer, another old Denver boy and now one of the country's top literary critics, working with Rewey Belle Inglis, now retired from active teaching but still one of the best of all the *Adventures* authors; Alice Cooper and Cecil Larson of California on *Adventures in English Literature.* A strong team working under an inspiring new young editor!

There was change, too, on the technical side of the 1952 *Adventures*. Bill wanted fresh creative thinking on the design side and so, instead of working with Robert Josephy, who had designed the *Adventures* series from its beginning in the twenties, he chose to work with Gerry Gross, a talented younger man in the Production Department. Strictly speaking, Gerry was the production man for trade books but we managed to get him to segregate a good chunk of time for the *Adventures*. He and Bill together did a great job in loosening up and livening up the old format.

By the early fifties I had taken over the informal supervision of production, after Don Brace's retirement. I was the one who could and did work most closely and successfully with Howard Clark, head of production. With gradually worsening health, Howard had become irritable and testy, a far cry from the sweet-natured person of his earlier years. Ordinarily, I would have expected a stiff contest for supervision over Howard from Dudley Meek, who was expanding his sphere of influence in these years. But Dudley, I figured, was content to leave a tartar like Howard to me, and sit on the sidelines, half expecting me to run into trouble. But my relationships with Howard were good enough that Gerry's aiding Bill Jovanovich on the 1952 *Adventures* worked smoothly.

Bill and Gerry engineered two innovations in the format of the series. They used a second color to brighten the inside. This was economically possible with the appearance at Plimpton Press of new presses that could print two colors simultaneously and hence at little increase in cost. Earlier, we had successfully used a second color—for the first time in any secondary school textbook—in a revised edition of *Your Health and Safety*. Incidentally, this was the first time one of our books was dummied. But the 1952 *Adventures* was the first high school literature series to use a second color, though two or even more colors had been used in elementary readers since Row Peterson first did so in 1938. The other eye-catching innovation was the use of brightly printed four-color photographs on the cloth of the covers. The 1952 *Adventures* really looked trail-blazing fresh!

Finally, there was one other simple shift. By the early fifties the revision numbers on the various anthologies had become bewildering: *Adventures in American Literature*, Third Edition, *Adventures in Appreciation*, Second Edition, and so on. This time, to clarify and ease reference to them and to stress the dramatic fact of simultaneous publication, we decided to give the 1952 edition a name instead of a bunch of numbers. I thought up the idea and Bill the actual name: *The Mer-cury Edition*. Each edition since has had its name: Olympic, Cardinal Newman, Laureate, Classic, Companion.

Bill introduced another innovation with the Mercury Edition: a parallel series of *Reading Workshops*, that is, workbooks to train and improve reading skills. By the early fifties a large expansion of school enrollments was beginning. This meant a less selective student body in the high school years, poorer training in reading in the elementary schools, and hence a demand in the high school for programs and materials to help train for better reading. Bill discovered Herbert Potell, a hard-working, rugged teacher of English and remedial reading in a Brooklyn high school and they worked together to produce the first *Reading Workshops*, a great help in putting the Mercury *Adventures* at the top.

All this time the Reids and the Jovanoviches were seeing—and enjoy-ing—each other socially: frequent cocktails, dinners, and bridge at each other's apartments. With promotions and salary increases Bill and Martha moved to better neighborhoods—and schools—first near the original location of the United Nations at Lake Success and later to a house in Westchester. One time Bill brought his father, who had come from his home in Denver for a visit, to cocktails at our apartment on Sutton Place. Jovanovich, Sr., was a marvelous man in his high fifties or low sixties and even more imposing physically, taller and more broad-shouldered, than Bill. A person of fine intelligence and integrity, he had been one of the leaders in the bloody Colorado Fuel and Iron Strike in 1912 and since then in the Slavic community in Denver.

Bill worked, I should say, an average of fifteen to sixteen hours a day on the Mercury *Adventures* and he got them out on schedule—in time for the Texas, Florida, and other adoptions—and soon they were on their way to the biggest sales yet and a widening lead over the com-petitors. Dudley Meek had the good sense to reward Bill with a month's vacation in Florida, but soon he was back working as hard as ever on a revision of *The World's History*, in addition to seeing through the seventh- and eighth-grade Mercuries and working with Paul Millane, our Catholic salesman, on the Cardinal Newman (Cath-olic) Edition of the *Adventures* series.

Paul Millane had come to us, as a salesman, in the late forties and by this time he had secured a clear mandate to start a Catholic Department; more expansion, starting with the Cardinal Newman Edition. The *Adventures* series had achieved a small but not-to-be-sneezed-at sale in the Catholic high schools in the forties and early fifties but we all realized the only way to make the business sizable was to offer a special Catholic Edition, edited by Catholic teachers. Paul Millane, a large, prematurely grey, and tense man in his thirties, led us to four strategically placed and able main Catholic editors and we signed them up. The adaptation consisted of eliminating some selections that were or might be offensive to Catholic sensibilities and the introduction of more Catholic authors and selections. Altogether, about 25% of each of the four anthologies was replaced or modified. On principle we did not include any strictly religious matter—with the full consent and collaboration of the Catholic editors. We didn't feel that we were making "concessions" but rather that we were making modifications to improve an already superior teaching instrument for a new and somewhat different audience. Not divisive, but cohesive: Catholic and public schools using *Adventures* anthologies would have 75% of their readings in literature in common. Using duplicate plates made from the original *Adventures* plates for three-quarters of the Cardinal Newman anthologies enabled us to keep the price competitive. Paul Millane hired a couple of Catholic salesmen and put on a strong campaign against L. W. Singer's Cathedral Edition, which had occupied the field almost alone. Our Cardinal Newmans took most of the Catholic literature business within a year or so.

In the meantime Dudley Meek was giving Emerson Brown—and sss and me—a tough time. It had almost become a pattern: I would have an idea. The idea would appeal to Dudley. He would take it over. Examples of this gall and wormwood: in the late forties I thought HB should have a pension plan and gained approval of the Board of Directors to start a study. Dudley, too, approved and pretty soon he was in there writing reports, making studies, and taking over. Inside the Textbook Department I had the idea for a fortnightly Editorial Round-Up, patterned somewhat after the old Round-Up of my high school club meetings. Pretty soon Dudley had expanded it to a Textbook Department Round-Up and had taken over the chairmanship.

Although only half aware of it at the time, I have come to think that AH and Dudley reached an understanding sometime in the late forties or early fifties that Dudley, with AH's support, would become the next president of HB. And Dudley began to act like the president more and more. Until this period Dudley had been most respectful of my editorial sovereignty, even after he had managed to get himself made head of the Textbook Department. As Bill Jovanovich gave more and more impressive demonstrations of his editorial abilities, Dudley became more and more bold, less exclusively dependent on me for the editorial power required for a great textbook organization. I never thought of Bill as my "successor" but rather as a strong younger partner, but I'm sure Dudley did.

In the early fifties Dudley's campaign took the form of harassing Emerson Brown in his work as social studies editor. In 1952 when Curtis Benjamin, president of McGraw-Hill, approached him, Emerson agreed to switch over and become head of McGraw-Hill's High School Department—without consulting me or SSS, or, as far as I know, anyone else at HB. Emerson was followed, in due course, by Norman Hunter, who had become a considerable sales powerhouse, first in New York State and then in California, but who was not on the best of terms with Lee Deighton, the general sales manager. Emerson's departure left a gap, hard to fill. Bill Jovanovich nobly stepped in and took over the editing of *The World's History*, at the time our most pressing problem. But Bill was already overworked.

In this period of the early fifties I myself was deep in the big job of getting out the seventh- and eighth-grade books to underpin the already fabulously successful ninth-grade book in the *Science for Better Living* series. And in the College Department, in addition to early work on Simpson's *Life*, I was engrossed in completing the editing of Hilgard's *Introduction to Psychology*. We had to launch it with a big splash to beat the dominant Scott Foresman rival. Both Hilgard and the two junior science books came out beautifully and went on to large successes.

At this time, too, I was working with Hy Ruchlis, a talented Brooklyn teacher discovered by Paul Brandwein, on *Exploring Physics*. This was not an easy editorial job and finally I brought in freelance William Gilmore to help in the re-write. Gilmore had done several re-write jobs for me, including the "unpurpling" of Odell Shepard's prose in the revision of the Shorter Edition of *The College Survey of English Literature*. Here was another spot where Dudley Meek conducted guerilla warfare. He was uncooperative and tried to make Gilmore's life miserable, as he, like many freelance writers, was in and out of unemployment compensation. Hampering Gilmore was indirectly hampering me. Also Dudley was, underneath, opposed to our publishing *any* physics book on the theory it was too small and insignificant a market to warrant the large expenditure of editorial time and considerable capital investment. Paul Brandwein and I, on the other hand, felt no publisher who aspired to become tops in science could afford to neglect or downgrade physics, most fundamental of the sciences. All in all, the early fifties were tough editorial years!

About this time, too, there occurred an unhappy and permanent break with Norman Maclean, my old friend and roommate. I had persuaded him and a talented colleague to undertake to prepare a MS for an *Introduction to Poetry*. Unfortunately, as it turned out, instead of editing it myself as would have been the natural move, I asked John McCallum to work with Maclean and his collaborator. After the first few chapters came in, John turned pretty negative on the project, saying it was "old hat," and he recommended we get out of it. Instead of taking the job back myself, I yielded to John's judgment and went to Maclean to ask that we call it quits. A man of sensitivity and pride, he of course made no resistance and the contract was cancelled. But I have always held myself guilty of an act of disloyalty to our ancient friendship and perhaps of a bad business decision! At any rate, things have never since been friendly between Norman and me.

A couple of physical afflictions began to add to the tension and distress of this span. In 1946, in a squash tennis tournament at the Yale Club, I had developed a limp. At first I thought it to be simply a pulled muscle, but as it gradually became worse, I gave up squash, shifting over to regular tennis, outdoors and indoors. Those were delightful years, playing at Elwood Cooke's Tudor City courts summers and at the Harlem Armory at 142nd Street and Fifth Avenue winters. The tennis companions of my wife Emmy and me were the poet Selden Rodman, Peter and Barbara Cary of *Reader's Digest*, and Ted and Mathilde Ferro, freelance radio writers. But by 1950 my limp had gotten so bad

I had to give up even tennis and—I thought—all sports. It turned out that my left hip had been damaged in the 1946 Yale Club accident and eventually I'd have to have the "hip" operation. In addition, the mounting conflicts and tensions in the office took another toll, in the form of an aggravating ulcer.

The publication and immediate success of the Hilgard and the junior high school *Science for Better Living* books early in 1953 marked a welcome high water mark. As a reward, Emmy and I took two months for a long-awaited trip to Europe—across to Naples on the great new liner *The Independence*, then to Rome, Venice, Florence, Lake Maggiore, Paris (even then somewhat hostile and a disappointment), and to Copenhagen, where Emmy's family (her aunts and uncles, and countless cousins) came to the airport, strewing our path with roses! We took them all to dinner at the great old hotel, the d'Angleterre. As we entered the main dining room, the courtly old orchestra in their swallowtails, recognizing that we were Americans, honored our entrance by playing, of all things, "Old Black Joe." Then on to a bonnie few days in ancestral Scotland and two great weeks of driving through Britain in an English Ford. The grand climax was a week in London, with theatre both nights and matinees. London theatre was even better than New York theatre, which we have always dearly loved. The housing of the London theatres was newer and more up-to-date than New York's; sixty-five to seventy shows to choose from; tickets, even for the hits, easy to get on short notice; more comfortable seating; drinks between the acts; the acting and production no better than New York's; but finally a precious sense of leisure and no sense of being pushed around. We had pleasant encounters with Frank Morley, by now freelancing it as author and editor, and Frank Chambers, now a lecturer in international relations at the London School of Economics and happily married, still enjoying good royalties on *This Age of Conflict*. Our return voyage on the *Caronia* brought us home to New York relaxed and happy. But not for long, as the struggle with Dudley came to a swift climax.

Only three weeks after our return to New York, Bill Jovanovich was put out of action by a severe heart attack. It came as a surprise since he was a young man, only thirty-three. But of course he worked strenuously, twelve to sixteen hours a day, often seven days a week, lots of coffee, and two, three, or four packs of cigarettes a day. It was a hard blow, for by now I had become most fond of Bill and it would take three good men to replace him in the editorial work of the School Department. His wife Martha telephoned me right after the attack came and I hastened out to see her in their home at Briarcliff Manor and him in the hospital. It was a narrow pull for Bill and months before he was anywhere near recovery. At one emotional moment I made a slip by saying to Bill that I felt almost like a father to him; but when I saw the resistance on his face, I corrected to what was a more accurate expression of the relationship: I looked on him as a younger brother. John McCallum was deeply frightened by Bill's heart attack, as he and Bill had become increasingly close in Bill's six years with HB. I really couldn't tell how Dudley Meek was affected; we were not in each other's confidence at this period.

Alfred Harcourt never met Bill, as far as I know. He did, however, with his wildly accurate intuition, say one time, "Harcourt, Brace & Jovanovich, maybe?" But AH's health had begun seriously to deteriorate and he had transferred his power and holdings to Hastings—with some unexpected results.

Hastings came East in the early fall of 1953. Somehow Dudley arranged to see him in Atlanta, as I remember it, before he got to New York. As I found out later from Hastings, whose habit it is to tell all, it was a stormy meeting. Dudley tried to set up a dominance over Hastings but this did not fit Hastings' self-image at all and served mainly to alienate him from Dudley permanently.

When Hastings arrived in New York, it became apparent that here was no carbon copy of AH but a young man who was going to do things *his* way, not necessarily his father's way. For one thing, Hastings had the noble idea of healing the long, sore breach between the Braces and the Harcourts. He made the friendliest of gestures to Don Brace, now in his early seventies. He even made overtures to Melville Cane, Don's great friend and advisor, and AH's chosen scapegoat.

Then one day John McCallum and I took Hastings to lunch at the Canadian Club, at the top of the Waldorf Astoria. The crux came suddenly when I suggested that the main block to good relations in the office and the constant source of plot and conflict was Dudley Meek.

Hastings said, "I'm not a Meek man" and told about the Atlanta meeting. Then John and I pulled out all stops, assuring Hastings that sss and Don Brace had been alienated by Dudley. With the welcome news that he (HH) was anti-Meek, the thing to do was to get Dudley—and possibly Lee Deighton, who had steadily sided with DM—out of the Company, despite his great ability and his large contributions to the building of the Textbook Department. John and I assured Hastings that the threesome of Reid, McCallum, and Jovanovich (recovered, hopefully) had the necessary talent and knowhow to underpin sss and enable HB not only to survive but to put on a growth spurt of massive magnitude once Meek was out. I took all this good news out to Briarcliff Manor and I'm confident it genuinely helped to speed Bill Jovanovich's recovery. Dudley, earlier—in August, as I recall—had also gone to see Bill and while I never knew what he said or what he offered Bill, I feared it meant little good for me. In any case, Bill and John and I agreed to work together through this fluid period.

Soon sss and Don Brace got the word that Hastings was anti-Meek and a coalition formed. Action came promptly. sss, with Hastings sitting by his side, simply called Dudley into his office and told him that he would like his resignation at once and stated that the Company would buy his stock and make what seemed at the time generous separation payments. sss said he wanted Dudley out of there at once. Then Lee Deighton was similarly called in and told. Lee said he wanted to stay, that he was not irrevocably tied to Dudley, and thought it unfair that he, too, had to leave simply because he was bracketed with Dudley. I personally felt it was a mistake to force Deighton out, for he was a man of enormous ability, despite an exterior that many (not I) found cold. Bill and John stood firmly for Deighton's ouster and their counsel prevailed.

Immediately after the two terse interviews, Dudley telephoned me and asked me to come to his office right away. I got up from a conference in the Production Department with Howard Clark and made the trek. Dudley, with Lee Deighton sitting at his side, said, "Jimmie, what do you know about these goings on?" I replied, "I know all about them and I am 100% for them." Lee said, "That's all I wanted to know. No more questions." But Dudley wanted to argue and discuss. I walked out of Dudley's office and never really talked to him again. After selling his stock, Dudley and his wife Helen went to Europe for a few months and after recovering from the shock of his ouster, he took a job at *Scholastic Magazine,* which didn't work out. He ended up on the staff of W. K. Jordan, the president of Radcliffe College, where, among other things, he did some good work in setting up courses in book publishing. Then in 1958, five years after leaving HB, he came down with lung cancer and, after a mercifully short illness, died.

It was otherwise with Lee Deighton. He held a series of jobs at various publishers, mainly editorial, specializing in reading improvement, and finally went to Macmillan, one of the large but slipping publishers, as head of their School Department, a job admirably suited to his talents. About this time my old friend from the Dissenters, Armand Erpf, of the big Wall Street investment banking firm of Loeb, Rhoades & Company, started operations in book publishing. Erpf told me that he was going to "build a publishing empire." His vehicle was the shaky Crowell Collier Company, which had just had to divest itself of *Collier's* and other magazines but had a large tax loss to carry over. Erpf began making acquisitions for Crowell Collier and perhaps the prize among them was Macmillan, ripe to fall out of the hands of the Brett family. I kept telling Erpf that the best man at Macmillan was Lee Deighton and eventually Deighton made his way up the ladder to the top post of Chairman of the Board.

The end of Dudley Meek at HB was not the end of the power struggle. But the Company was stronger, by far, and ready for a great leap ahead. AH in his final sickness . . . Don Brace retired, though he came to the office every day . . . SSS wondering if he could ride all the wild horses and already thinking about his own retirement . . . Hastings strong but jumpy . . . Bill Jovanovich, John McCallum, and I with the most ambitious plans for the Company and for ourselves . . . Surely all this marked the beginnings of something big!

CHAPTER EIGHT

INTO ORBIT

(1954-1960)

THE DEPARTURE OF MEEK AND DEIGHTON WAS, as it turned out, merely the first of several struggles before a new and stable structure emerged. But HB was no more riven by deep differences than the nation itself was in 1954, the height of the Senator Joe R. McCarthy era. What a climate! What terrible things went on in the early fifties!

Before the '52 campaign began, Truman was clearly through and a big change from the policies of FDR, Truman, and the New Deal was inevitable. Even a wonderful strong liberal like Jack Hilgard, long active in the American Civil Liberties Union in California, said he thought it would be good for the country if the Republicans won. He thought Eisenhower might bring much-needed unification to the country. Adlai Stevenson made his comet-like but mistimed appearance. A fine human being and a superb deliverer of political eloquence! But Eisenhower swept in on the slogan "I will go to Korea and end this terrible conflict." He did end the war but his "unifying" of the country was more like surrender to reaction.

Rough-riding Senator Joe McCarthy overrode all opposition. His ruthless young assistants, Roy Cohn and G. David Schine, strutted and overcame here and overseas. Few other senators dared to oppose him, for to oppose was to be branded an ally of Alger Hiss and a subversive in league with the Communists, who, according to McCarthy, infested the whole Federal Government. The State Department was badly damaged by his attacks and insinuations, and even the Army hardly dared to stand up to him. We all cheered the senators (notably McClelland of Arkansas, Symington of Missouri, Jackson of Washington) who formed a belated opposition to the McCarthy investigations and did finally do battle. There were blacklists in radio and TV as the McCarthy poison spread. Nixon was using "guilt by association" to win elections in California and make his way up the political ladder.

Simultaneously with McCarthy was the Chambers-Hiss episode, which effectively destroyed much of the left-liberal-moderate sentiment in the country. Like all my friends and associates, I was deeply interested in the deadly struggle between Chambers and Hiss. It was futile to try—still is—to get to its murky bottom. But Chambers made little sense to me, while Hiss did make some. I was glad many years later to help give employment as a copyeditor in the School Department to Priscilla Hiss, his divorced wife. And there is a possibly apocryphal story about Mr. Welch, the wonderful old Boston attorney who finally gave McCarthy his comeuppance in the dramatic Army-McCarthy hearings nationally broadcast in the spring of '54.

The story concerns the hiring of Welch and it comes from Paul Todd, the author, with Merle Curti, of our top-selling senior high school textbook, *America's History*. Todd lives on Cape Cod not far from Welch's summer home on the Cape. One stormy night, there was a knock on the door of the Todd house. Todd opened the door, recognized Joseph Welch from his TV appearances, and invited him in. In the course of the conversation and a couple of drinks, Welch told how he was hired to battle McCarthy in the Senate hearings in Washington.

One day—apparently in the spring of '54—one of Welch's law partners asked Welch, with an air of mystery, to go to New York on a certain date, proceed to the Hotel Commodore, and knock on the door of a certain room at a certain hour. He would find there someone who wanted to talk to him in strictest secrecy on a matter of national urgency. Welch, though mystified, complied, and knocked on the prescribed door at the Commodore. He was ushered into a suite where sat Tom Dewey, still a great power in the Republican Party, and friend of my friend Lowell Thomas. Paul and I have always thought that Dewey was acting not only for himself and other big shots in the GOP but probably even for President Eisenhower in securing Welch for a belated but eventually successful counterattack on McCarthy.

I was able to take in—on TV at our apartment on Sutton Place—the dramatic, climactic week of the Army-McCarthy hearings, in which Welch finally destroyed McCarthy. I was having a week off from the office in May of '54 to scout around and decide whether to stay at HB or to start my own publishing business. A whole series of exciting struggles had led up to my week of exploration.

Alfred Harcourt was in his illness of terminal cancer in California and died there in June, 1954 at the age of 73. Donald Brace died, also of cancer, in September of 1955 at the age of 73, but he was still active throughout 1954 and much of 1955. In fact, Don was the pivot in setting up the succession at HB.

Soon after the departure of Meek and Deighton, Bill Jovanovich swiftly recovered much of his strength and health. The coalition of three—Bill, John McCallum, and supposedly headed by me as senior partner—soon fell apart. It was, like any *troika* or committee set-up, a weak arrangement, as Don Brace was quick to point out. At one very dramatic meeting at Bill Jovanovich's house in Briarcliff Manor, Bill, speaking for himself and John, asked to be released from our half-articulated "committee" arrangement, saying that if I said "*No*," he and John would still honor it. I did agree to step down as "chairman," John did a wild little dance, and we all went with our wives to dinner and many drinks at a nearby hostelry. On the train home that night, I recanted and soon found myself allied with sss, confronting Bill, John, and Hastings. A power struggle of some length ensued. Donald Brace held the balance of power.

Throughout this struggle, I never seriously considered myself a leading candidate to succeed sss as president of HB. For one thing, sss himself indicated he would not advance my cause. And Don Brace, as in 1940 when he rushed Frank Morley in to block Hastings and incidentally and less importantly to block my appointment as trade editor-in-chief, stood firmly against it. And finally, Hastings not only was never at any time a Reid advocate but was actively pushing Jovanovich and McCallum swiftly along.

Initially, sss and I had, on the surface at least, a strong position. sss was president and chief executive officer. He had just shown his strength by firing Meek. I was editor-in-chief of both High School and College Departments, a director of the corporation, and secretary. But soon Bill and John were made directors and after a short interval, both were made vice-presidents. Bill became head of the High School Department and John became head of the College Department. There never was a very clear definition of authority between the two heads on the one hand and the editor-in-chief on the other.

Soon there were skirmishes. For example, I assigned Jack Gallagher, who had mainly edited in the College Department, to work on a high school MS without consulting Bill or John. It needed the kind of close editing and re-write that Jack could furnish. sss never did settle the differences between the members of the old *troika*. The skirmishes went on and sss began to think of his retirement and what kind of a deal he could make for his retirement pay. He had steadily refused to join the rest of us in the Company-wide retirement plan.

There was one dramatic confrontation—Bill and John talking against me—in a night session of the directors at the Columbia Club. Here we aired our differences. John made what I thought was a narrow speech, Bill a broad and eloquent one, and I made one which Don Brace described as "saintly." In it I told how I could never work for John, as I did not consider him as good an all-around publisher as I was; but I did say that I could work for Bill because I considered him in a number of ways to be as good or better a man than I was. A more fluent writer, he also had a larger capacity for turning out the work! From this point on, the winds blew Jovanovich. Mainly, Bill impressed Don Brace that he had the presidential stuff and with Hastings' backing already, and sss visibly wanting to make the best possible deal for his own retirement, wij became the obvious choice.

Bill's big stroke in the skirmishing with me was to put over the idea that the two departments, High School and College, had gotten too big to share just one editor-in-chief. Don Brace had Melville Cane, his friend and my lawyer who a decade earlier had seen me through the divorce of my first wife, tell me this decision. I was told by Melville I had the choice of being chief editor of either department, but I had to give up one of them. It was at this point that I took a week off to think and to explore going it alone.

Finally, I decided to keep the High School Department job. Here was the place of greatest possible growth; here the inside editor had more impact on the product than on college MSS; and altogether I felt

even more at home in the high school work than I did in the college
duties. But I did not feel sure that I was really wanted in the High
School Department. So I went to Don Brace and he was quick to tell
me that I was truly wanted there. Bill sought me out quickly and said,
"You are the best editor I know. I do very much want you." So
that's the way it was. I stayed, though if I had been forty-two instead
of fifty-two, I might well have tossed my hat over the windmill and
tried to set up the J. M. Reid Company.

By the fall of 1954 sss had made a financially attractive retirement
deal with Don and Hastings, but the price was his immediate retirement
at age sixty-two. Bill Jovanovich was his successor and for HB the publishing stratosphere became the challenge. No more were there sss's
cautious, modest policies. Instead WJ's vaulting imagination and disciplined energies. And in the change from WIJ to WJ lies a story.

Not only did Bill drop the middle initial after becoming president of
HB, but he remodeled himself in several ways. He became more careful
and conservative of his dress and more frequent with the haircuts. Not
that he had ever been careless about either. He joined the Union League
Club, high meeting place of New York conservatives and a far cry
politically from the young man who, only six years earlier, had voted
for Henry Wallace's third party.

Hastings became chairman of the board when WJ became president.
But longtime observers of Hastings wondered how long he could stick
to it. Hastings was great on the quick intuitions but he never could
concentrate very long on anything. He set himself up in a good-sized office at 383 Madison Avenue and furnished it in the grand manner. He was
always drifting down the aisle to burst in and consult WJ and it was
this annoying practice, I suspect, which brought his regular presence
in the office to an end. WJ simply "fired" him as chairman of the board,
not as director, and asked him to please return to Santa Barbara. A
bold move, which I never would have had the nerve for, but WJ did
it and made it stick!

Soon after "inauguration," heads began to fall. First to go was Gene
Reynal as vice-president and head of the Trade Department. Actually,
Gene had played but a minor role in all the power struggles of 1953-54
and soon Bill and John felt they could do better. Shortly after, Robert
Giroux, editor-in-chief of the Trade Department, and by now a valu-

able and fully developed editor, left—in some disgust—to become editor-in-chief at Farrar & Straus, and eventually a full partner at Farrar,
Straus, & Giroux. He simply could not stomach the over-dramatic
maneuvers, he told me, of John and Bill in establishing their dominance over Trade. With him went T. S. Eliot, Thomas Merton, and a
full dozen other trade authors. Denver Lindley, another respected trade
editor, left for Viking in due course, too. But Margaret McElderry,
the able head of the Juvenile Department, stayed solid. Bill Vickery,
a Meek man, left the comptroller job, despite wj's desire to keep him,
for a well-paid spot in the advertising business.

We were all in agreement that HB and especially the High School and
College Departments were ready to be unleashed for big expansion. wj
was quick to make Burnett Ball the general sales manager of the High
School Department. Just before the Meek-Deighton debacle in '53,
Meek had begun to cut Ball, manager of the Chicago office, down to
the size he thought Ball should be, saying Ball was a good salesman but
a poor administrator with various defects which DM could so plausibly
present. wj reversed all this and enabled Ball, through solid backing
and a show of real confidence, to blossom out and develop his poten-
tial; he became the greatest textbook salesman of the middle twentieth
century. In turn, Ball's growth released the full energies of his two
good younger men, Charles Murphy and Dick Manatt, only slightly
less potent in sales than Ball himself. I enjoyed a particularly close
relationship with Murph, who was aware of what made a textbook
sell and uncanny in his sensitivity—usually before anyone else—to
sales slippages and what was causing them. Murph was just about my
best editorial "litmus paper"! Another one, later in the decade, was
Carl Procasky, our Michigan man; he was written up as the "model"
salesman in *The American School Book*, a trade book by Hillel Black
(Morrow) in the mid-sixties.

About this time, too, Paul Millane felt the urge for further and
greener fields. He left our Catholic Department, which he had founded,
and wound up eventually as head of Scribner's nearly moribund School
Department. wj hired a talented and delightful successor, Leonard
Sullivan, a star example of the intelligent and disciplined Catholic, who
came on to do a great job for HB. Len and I always worked together
with the greatest mutual respect—and success.

Strong and able women had always been an important part of the smooth functioning of the HB organization. At this stage, WJ fastened onto Margaret Mary McQuillan, who had risen to head of the girls in the High School Department and made her his efficient good secretary. She was succeeded by Gwen Kerr, whom I soon grabbed—at WJ's suggestion—as my top secretary. I had always been a two-secretary man and Gwen surely was about the best I ever had. Though Lisa Mayer, the number-two girl who came to me from my friend Bill Lawrence of the Boy Scouts when they made the mistake of moving to New Jersey, was loyal and good. Shades of Frances Reilly, Rose Kuchta, Dorothy Mott, and Mariana Ball will rise up to haunt this paragraph!

Howard Clark's death preceded the power struggles of 1954 by only a few weeks and the Production Department badly needed an infusion of new blood. Kermit Patton, whom I had been building up and helping along in Howard's last few years, was ready to step in as head of production. But talented Gerry Gross slipped away to another company, where he became an editor as well as production head. And Bob Josephy retired from designing books to become a successful apple farmer in Connecticut. In quick succession—the Reid luck holding strong in the hiring—we acquired two greatly talented book designers: Stanley Rice, son of a Dartmouth economics professor and one of the most original designers in the industry, came to us from freelancing and found at HB a ready and sympathetic outlet for his ideas; and Meyer (Mike) Miller, a complete production man and himself a designer of parts, came without too much persuasion from Macmillan.

At the same time I hastened the growth of our high school copyediting department, which forms a close liaison between editorial and production. Grace Carlson had come to us from rival Scott Foresman in the forties and in the early fifties had begun to train, expand, and improve our bank of copyeditors. Copyediting became, in fact, a fertile proving ground for good female editors, most notably Dorothy Snowman (High School) and Mildred Boxhill (College).

In the College Department, WJ and John McCallum added some manpower, notably editor Bill Pullin (from Prentice-Hall) and Bill Tackett, a protégé of my great friend and *Adventures* author, Mary Bowman. Soon there was a kind of contest going between Pullin and Paul Corbett for the headship of the College Department. Corbett won out, adding a large growth of editorial knowhow to his fine sales background. But it was four or five years before College developed good-selling "post-Reid" books and began its big spurt.

Among the important new people was George L. White in promotion. George came to us when Silver Burdett dropped its New York office and moved its whole operation to Morristown, deep in New Jersey. George is one of the few in textbooks at HB with a Ph.D. He had acquired it at the University of Pennsylvania after his undergraduate career at Amherst, and a few years of college English teaching. He became High School promotion head, taking the place of level-headed and versatile Cameron Moseley, who moved up to become Eastern sales manager and later business manager. George worked out a promotion set-up that could handle a big flow of sales and advertising propaganda. In the middle fifties WJ persuaded George to have a fling at the post of editor-in-chief of the Trade Department, but after a short regime there, we were glad to have him back in the High School Department. Actually I pitched in and did all I could to help George in Trade. John Scott's *Democracy Is Not Enough,* Frank Hercules' *The Flight of the Humming Bird,* and Robert Bendiner's *Whitehouse Fever* came out under George's administration, all three my boys from the Dissenters. Among George's talents are a superior public speaking ability, which Ball made good use of in state adoption campaigns—and the ability to hit a golf ball in the low seventies! The other two top golfers in HB are Ed Hodge of Trade and Stan Rice of Production. We common editors, salesmen, and executives seem to be too high-strung to score well in the ancient and difficult game which the Scots, with their uncanny knowledge of all the weaknesses of human nature, invented. Subsequently, they invented whiskey to enable their victims to recover from the self-inflicted wounds of golf!

I found High School Editorial depleted of its extraordinary and talented manpower: WJ gone upstairs, Lee Deighton into the wide world, Emerson Brown to McGraw-Hill. First thing we did was to send for Newbury Morse and persuade him to give up his New England territory, move his family to the New York area, and devote full time to editing. This he did at some sacrifice of congenial social context in his home just outside Boston, but he arrived just in time to help us keep a number of important projects moving. Then I hired a good young man, James S. Russell, son of a Presbyterian minister, who came in through Art English of Plimpton Press and Jim soon developed into a superb English editor. I always think of him as my true successor. Shortly thereafter I hired two other talented young men: Joseph V. Sheehan and Adrian Sanford. Both turned out to be exceptionally productive English editors. Joe left us to join Addison Wesley, a rising new textbook house, and in 1969 became vice-president and editor-in-chief of its school division. Adrian came to me in 1961, telling me he was resigning to start his own firm back home in Palo Alto, California. I argued (wrongly) against this move, as I did not think that Adrian, though he was one of my best editors, had the business acumen to start, organize, and run an educational publishing business. He went ahead anyway and today is chairman of the board of Educational Development Corporation, a prosperous young company that has just recently "gone public." It prepares "editorial packages" for a variety of publishers, who then print, promote, and sell Adrian's "packages."

Then Donald McGregor Stewart came in looking for a job as social studies editor. wj was for hiring him pronto, for he had obvious ability and a record of great achievement in textbook editing. A graduate of Brown University in the middle thirties, he had gone after graduation via the distinguished Scott Foresman editor, Lindsay Todd Damon, who was also professor of English at Brown, to join the Scott Foresman editorial staff. There he edited their great history of civilization book for colleges, Wallbank and Taylor, and their equally great college handbook of English by Perrin, a perennial rival of Hodges' *Harbrace Handbook*. But Don began to have troubles; then came a series of other jobs, most of them good: writer on *Fortune* magazine, and at Stanford University Press, where he edited and published a book on the Constitution which sold in the hundreds of thousands. Most impressive, he had worked several years at Houghton Mifflin and produced for them their two big-selling American histories. The one for the eighth-grade put a crimp in the sales of our Casner and Gabriel. I hired Don and he has turned in a remarkable performance in bringing the HB social studies list to the top of the industry in less than ten years.

Another good man came in through sales: Don E. Meyer, an Oklahoma boy who was a good salesman but soon showed he had the editorial touch in science and mathematics. And Dorothy Snowman came up through copyediting to become one of our very best English editors. Marian Lovrien, a superb teacher of English in Chicago, had collaborated with Herbert Potell on our Track Two *Adventures* series. I persuaded her that her best future lay in editing English books for us. Fortunately, this suggestion coincided with her plan to get married to Earl Miller, leave Chicago, and come to New York with her new husband. All in all, a fine new crop of editors.

Nicely re-tooled at the end of the Senator Joe McCarthy outrage, the death of Stalin (another world landmark), and the time of maximum internal struggles at HB, we found ourselves in the quieter, slightly suffocating humid atmosphere of Eisenhower, Nixon, and the two Dulles. Perhaps some wounds did heal, as Jack Hilgard hoped, in these years of inactivism, even dullness (or Dullesness!), on the college campuses. The country as a whole seemed sodden rather than recuperating. It took successive shocks of the twin crises of Suez and the brutal crushing of the Hungarian revolt in 1956, followed by Sputnik in 1957, and the coming of Kennedy in 1960 to rouse us up.

Beginning in November of 1954, I personally had a long year (thirteen months) of the surgeon's knife, which slowed me down temporarily. First, Dr. Sam Standard, great surgeon and lover of soprano opera singers, supplemented by our own Dr. Irving Newman, took out a large ulcer, which rightly or wrongly I have chiefly blamed on Dudley Meek and the terrible infighting he instituted in 1948. Then, in May of 1955, when my stomach had nicely knitted and I was able to take whiskey again in comfort, my left hip got just too painful and I had to have "the hip operation." This was a fairly new operation, having been developed at the Hospital for Special Surgery in the late forties. It was performed by Dr. T. Campbell Thompson, head of the hospital, another great surgeon but lacking in Dr. Sam's human warmth. I was on crutches for sixteen months, then on a cane for about three years. But finally I found myself carrying, rather than using, my cane. And so I threw it away; the residue is a slight limp and a left leg that has never quite recovered its full strength. This hip operation meant the end of all athletics except bowling—and golf.

In the spring of '58 while on a transcontinental MS trip, I stopped off in Des Moines for a weekend with my sister Miriam. She said come, let's play nine holes. I said don't be absurd—I can't walk nine holes. She said try it with an electric golf cart. We did the nine holes with help of the cart and I returned to Connecticut to tell my wife Emmy that we were joining the Waccabuc Country Club, buying a golf cart, and she was learning to play golf. Moral: never underestimate the recuperative powers of a human body that is treated with even a little respect. Now ended thirteen months of doctors and hospitals, and I returned full time to the office at HB, 383 Madison Avenue.

Paul Brandwein was going strong as our general editor in science. We signed up Arthur Greenstone of Brooklyn for high school chemistry, but he needed collaborators. We had such difficulty over the years in getting the right combination on this project that it took more than ten years to get the MS written and the book, originally *Exploring Chemistry* but finally *Concepts in Chemistry*, through the works.

An even more exciting science project was *The Physical World*, a pioneering textbook in physical science. We designed it to have a low mathematical content and a broad coverage of physics, chemistry, and the other physical sciences. We planned it originally for students in the upper grades of the high school who do not have the interest or the ability to do well in the standard (and difficult) science courses. Unexpectedly, as it turned out, the book came to have a respectably good sale, lower down, to the "fast" or superior sections of ninth-grade general science.

But *The Physical World* was only one example of a strong, swift-growing trend, which we at HB were early to sense: the need for special text materials for the variously called "slower" student: the reluctant reader (a phrase that I started), the disadvantaged, the Track Two student, the non-academic pupil, and so on. In science we soon added *Your Biology* by Ella Thea Smith and Lorenzo Lisonbee, of Phoenix, Arizona. It was eighth-grade reading level (two grades below normal), its content broken into one- or two-day lessons, short easy bites to fit the short attention span of the non-academic student, and heavily illustrated for strong visual appeal—that was our formula.

In parallel development we sought to enrich the various courses and the teaching equipment by furnishing a variety of aids: film strips, recordings, teaching tests, and, later, paperbacks for supplementary reading.

It was my policy personally to carry the ball in our ventures into new and unexplored fields. Partly it was a selfish policy, for I thoroughly enjoyed the challenge of the new and unknown. But also, if a strange new project had the imprimatur of the editor-in-chief, it would have a better chance not only in attracting and signing up the requisite creative talent but also in gaining the attention and support of our salesmen.

Dudley Meek had successfully blocked Paul Brandwein's and my plan to prepare film strips to accompany the *Science for Better Living* books, but WJ was quick to encourage me to revive the project. So Paul and Don Meyer (then a neophyte science editor) and I plunged into the preparation of a set of nine film strips for the ninth-grade general science book, one film strip for each of the nine units. We had the professional help of Irving Milgate, who had prepared many film strips for my friend Bill Lawrence, director of training for the Boy Scouts of America, who originally stirred my interest in film strips. We strongly believed the film strip had many teaching advantages over motion pictures. For one thing it is completely under the control of the teacher, who can stop and discuss or lecture or supplement at any point, whereas the motion picture carries with it a compulsion to completion and is hard to handle in an informal classroom situation. Also, it's easier to gain active student participation in a film strip than in a motion picture, which just naturally calls forth the responses associated with passive entertainment. We did some good pioneering here, but the time was not yet, for the sales were disappointing. Only in the mid-sixties did HB return to the making of film strips in a large way, by acquiring Guidance Associates, which became a productive division of the Company.

The substantial increase of slow or disadvantaged students in the high schools of the fifties was a part, of course, of the swelling enrollments which followed after the usual number of months and years the return of the men from fighting World War Two. It called forth, as I have just indicated, new and special text materials. Correspondingly, it created a demand for greatly increased teaching staff. In response, experienced teachers and teachers who had retired upon marriage came out of retirement to be retreaded, the teachers colleges and "normal schools" (as they used to be called) tried to speed up and enlarge. Nevertheless, teaching quality deteriorated. Many poorly or partly trained teachers infiltrated the secondary schools. We at HB soon felt pressure to do what we could to have our text materials and teaching aids take over part of the burden. And so, for the first time at HB, we seriously undertook to provide teachers' manuals for our main books.

Up until this time, my editorial policy had always been to build all messages to the teacher, including those on how to teach the textbook, into the textbook itself. We addressed our "teaching" messages directly to the student on the theory the teacher would have to read anything addressed to the student. We figured, rightly for secondary school teaching in the twenties, thirties, and forties, that high school teachers rarely would even read, much less accept the guidance of a teachers' manual. Also, I claimed, the textbook author who was deprived of communicating through a teachers' manual would be challenged to write it all directly to the student and thereby do a better job on the textbook itself. But the big influx of students, larger classes, and teaching staffs of diluted quality changed all this and we at HB became aware of a new responsibility to help the schools by furnishing teachers' manuals.

Perhaps we would have had an easier time of it if we had had the experience of an elementary school list of textbooks, where teachers' manuals and/or teachers' editions are normal procedure and have been for years. To us, teachers' manuals were a big—and expensive—innovation. In addition to working with an author on the main text to get it out on schedule, the textbook editor now had to plan a whole extra book of two hundred to four hundred or so pages and educate his author to write the manual, as well as see the main textbook through the works—all this, hopefully, on the same high-pressure schedule. Especially in series like the *Adventures,* where we now were determined to gain or retain the sales advantage of simultaneous publication of all the books in the series and all the satellites (tests, film strips, records, etc.) the teachers' manuals made for an editorial logjam of mammoth proportions. It required more editorial manpower—and fast.

All this meant increase in editorial costs and I was the one to work out changes in the pricing formula which would enable us to recover our new, increased expenditures. Few people, I think, realized I had this special and slightly mathematical interest in business formulas, but I did. Back in the early thirties I had worked out a formula for compensating salesmen in proportion to their sales increases but allowing for the varying sales resistances of territories. My formula, which attracted the support of sss, aroused the long-term enmity of Dudley Meek.

After the large success of the Mercury *Adventures* and wj's elevation to the presidency, I took back the job of directing the next revision of the series—the Olympic *Adventures*. With teachers' manuals for the first time, accompanying albums of records for the first time, the *Reading Workshops* for each of the six grades, and *Test Booklets* —all for simultaneous publication in 1958—it was a big and exciting job. Naturally I was determined to show that the founder of the *Adventures* series could still get one up, not only over competitors but over wj and his Mercuries, the best to date.

It was a most interesting necessity—to put together strong and fast teams of authors outside the office, editors, and design-production people inside the office, altogether 132 people—to produce the Olympic *Adventures*. It was a far cry from the early days of the first *Adventures* in the twenties—and a far cry from the titanic, practically one-man effort by wj on the Mercury *Adventures* in the early fifties. I venture to think that my Olympic *Adventures* procedures set the new pattern at HB for putting important big series through the works.

For each of the six grades I organized a team: two or three outside authors for the selection hunting, original writing, and the teaching knowhow; a designer-production expert for superior design, color, and layout, and to work with an average of twelve outside artists per anthology; a copyeditor to take care of the housekeeping details; and an inside editor personally to do the editing, coordinate the work of all the others, and shepherd the anthology and its satellites through the works as expeditiously as possible—and on schedule! For each grade we had to produce the following:

> the main anthology, ranging from 608 double-column pages for grade seven to the fattest of them all, the eleventh-grade book of 864 double-column pages;
> a Reading Workshop with Tests, 160 pages;

a Teacher's Manual, 228 pages; and

a Many Voices album of one or two 33-1/3 rpm 12" records for each anthology.

All this adds up to a grand total of 4500 pages of anthology, 640 pages of Reading Workshop, 1368 pages of Teacher's Manual, and nine long-play records for seven and one-half hours of listening. It would be vulgar to divulge the amount of capital HB poured into the Olympic *Adventures*, but anyhow the dollar figures would be an understatement. For the blood, sweat, and extra hours from us all escape precise measurement.

New members of the author group included some interesting characters:

ELIZABETH D. O'DALY, a Brooklyn junior high school principal and head of New York's Curriculum Planning Committee for Junior High Schools. No panel really complete without a good, tough (and sensitive) Irishman or two.

MARJORIE BRAYMER, Sequoia High School in Redwood City, California. On one of my MS trips in the early fifties, Mary Bowman of Texas and an *Adventures* author since 1940 put me onto Marge. When I barged into her classroom at Sequoia, we recognized each other as old friends and co-workers in the Book and Magazine Guild in New York of the middle thirties. Marge had won the Vandewater Poetry prize at Ohio State in 1943 and later wrote *The Walls of Windy Troy*, a good-selling biography of the great German archeologist, Heinrich Schliemann, which our Trade Department published in the early sixties.

DOROTHY HOLMSTROM of Illinois, Nebraska, and Colorado, a true voice of the vital mid-section of the nation, and a teacher of teachers as well as a teacher of high school students. I had a pet theory that a big-selling book had to hit the breadbasket (Midwest) right in the middle.

JOSEPHINE SPEAR, head of the English Department at the Indiana University High School, came in to understudy Rewey Belle Inglis, who with John Gehlman were the only survivors of the original *Adventures* authorship, recruited by Harry Schweikert, sss, and me back in the twenties.

B. Jo KINNICK, teacher of English and creative writing at the Oakland High School in California, was another newcomer who came in at first to help Herb Potell with the Reading Workshops and the rest of us with the Teacher's Manuals. She was also a poet, minor to be sure, but nevertheless a good and true poet.

In addition to new blood in the *Adventures* authorship for the Olympic Edition we recruited some fresh glamor from the worlds of literature, TV, the theatre, and Hollywood for the gay and splashy "picture essays" which we put in to introduce each anthology:

MARY MARTIN, of stage and movie and TV fame, for grade eight

JESSE STUART, the Kentucky bard and fecund short story writer, for grade nine

JESSAMYN WEST, the Quaker novelist and short story writer, for grade ten

CLIFTON FADIMAN, versatile critic and host on radio and TV, for grade eleven

J. B. PRIESTLEY, the great English playwright and novelist, for grade twelve

Several of these distinguished and creative people doubled as commentators on the *Many Voices* records.

Clifton Fadiman I had known from the thirties, the years of the Book and Magazine Guild and the time of his service as editor at Simon and Schuster. It was good to be working with him on *Adventures in American Literature:* Olympic Edition. But the business relations, all with his brother who functioned as his agent, were pretty repulsive. The Fadimans just could not believe that I was not only fair but considerably on the low side when estimating probable royalty earnings. Throughout my career as textbook editor, relations with literary agents were fortunately rare, for the ones I did have, with an occasional exception (notably Bernice Baumgarten of Brandt & Brandt), I can only say were repulsive. I hope the agents will keep out of the textbook part of the industry. Kip Fadiman several years later did admit that he'd got good treatment and royalty payments far beyond his expectations from HB.

There is one unsavory episode concerning the Olympic *Adventures* I must tell—the bitter along with the sweet. Henry Steele Commager, the great writer of American history and a fine literary critic, was originally one of the authors for the Olympic *Adventures in American Literature*, the eleventh-grade book and consistently not only the bestseller of the series but also the best-selling textbook of HB. Henry Commager is my own age and, along with the political scientist and columnist Max Lerner, a member of what Max and I call "The Class of 1902," the year we were born. Early in the preliminary work on the Olympics, Henry invited Mary Bowman, John Gehlman, and me to his house in Vermont for a delightful long weekend of talk and planning. Over the next couple of years he did his part as promised, writing a new and fresh history of American life and literature to replace the one by Wil Schramm, which with minor polishing and adjustments had served so well through three editions. Then, a year or so before publication, the sales department, especially Burnett Ball, the general sales manager, and King Burney, the top Texas man, got panicky. There was still some Senator Joe McCarthy poison in the American social system and they were afraid of Commager's well-known liberal position. They did not object to anything in the history that Commager wrote for *Adventures in American Literature;* they said his name as an author on the title page would permit competitors to do some dirty infighting and harm their chances in state adoptions, especially in the South. It was an agonizing decision and I finally felt I had to give in. I had to persuade Henry Commager to permit us to use his history without using his name and of course at no reduction of his royalty. Not only were the royalties and sales of the eleventh-grade book at stake but also those of the other books in the series, for "AmLit" was the pivotal book. I made the "right decision" for sales and royalties (echoes of Alfred Harcourt: "No point in publishing a good book if nobody buys it") but a smelly one for the integrity of the series and of HB. It's wrong when the names of the true and responsible authors do not appear on the title pages of textbooks. After this, Henry Commager bore little good feeling toward me or HB.

In addition to getting J. B. Priestley to write the literary history for *Adventures in English Literature,* by far the best history the book has ever had, our great coup was to include the complete text of *Pygmalion,* the first time ever for a George Bernard Shaw play to be presented in an American school anthology. Shaw himself never permitted anthologizing of his plays but when the old boy finally died (at ninety-one!), we were able to go through regular channels and persuade Dodd Mead, his American publisher, to use their influence, plus our good money offer, with the Shaw estate to come through with the requisite permission to reprint. Great good fortune—or the Reid luck!—attended us, for publication of Olympic "E Lit" coincided with the appearance on Broadway of *My Fair Lady*, an instant and long-lived smash hit. Every English teacher that came to New York had to see *My Fair Lady* and return to her classroom full of good teaching supplements for *Pygmalion*, which became a durable—and endurable—classic of the classroom, nearly as great and long-lived as Thornton Wilder's *Our Town*, which festooned our "AmLit" from 1942 on.

Perhaps the most fun of the Olympics was the putting together of the nine *Many Voices* recordings. I can't claim them as the first set of recordings specially prepared to accompany a literature series. The conservative and unimaginative American Book Company (of all the competitors!) was the first. It led the way in the early fifties; it had some help from my old friend Louis Untermeyer, who in this decade was working at Decca Records. It was one of our quiet but effective salesmen from the Chicago office, Bill Moogk, who first let me know that the ABC recordings had hurt him in Indiana. He urged me to get us records to go with the Olympic *Adventures*. I went to Louis Untermeyer to find out how to do it and he in turn led me to Arthur Luce Klein, a free-lance producer of oral and literary recordings, and former Professor of Speech and Drama at the Universities of California and Michigan. A grand person to work with.

First step was to assemble a sort of "record cabinet," consisting of:

JIM RUSSELL for *Adventures for Readers*, Books One and Two
JIM MILHOLLAND for *Adventures in Reading* and *Adventures in Appreciation*
MARIAN MILLER for *Adventures in American Literature*
DOROTHY SNOWMAN for *Adventures in English Literature*
ARTHUR LUCE KLEIN, producer
THE EDITOR-IN-CHIEF (me)

We met mostly after the usual business hours and the first thing we did was to listen to the American Book Company records and consider how we could improve them, good pioneering effort though they were.

We decided we wanted to present substantial units for classroom listening, on the assumption that most English teachers would prefer to devote a whole class period to literary readings, rather than little piecemeal offerings *a la* American Book Company. Otherwise, it would be hard to justify the extra trouble of getting the school record player wheeled into the English classroom and set for playing. We planned each unit for about eight or nine minutes of listening so three units would occupy one side of a longplay record, about twenty-four to twenty-six minutes of listening. Thus we allowed on days of listening to *Many Voices* fifteen to twenty minutes for class discussion and the mechanics of the English period, which is, on the average, forty-five minutes long. A typical unit is Unit V: "Our Home: the Earth" from *Many Voices* 4A, for the tenth-grade book, *Adventures in Appreciation:*

A short introduction by the narrator, Richard Wilbur, the young poet-teacher from Wesleyan University, and Pulitzer Prize-winner

Readings by e. e. cummings, one of our major lyrical poets, of four short poems:
"What Is So Rare as a Day in June" by James Russell Lowell
"Spring Thunder" by Mark Van Doren
"To a Snowflake" by Francis Thompson
"in Just—" by e. e. cummings

Reading by Carl Sandburg of his "Four Preludes on Playthings of the Wind"

All selections appear in the anthology and it is assumed that the class has studied them and got the sense of the selection *before* listening. The *Many Voices* recordings give finished performances by skilled readers of poetry or by the poets themselves and thus enrich the course. However, some teachers preferred the opposite, that is, to use the recordings to *introduce* the selection and motivate study.

We went to great lengths to secure recordings by the poets themselves: Sandburg came to our studio and recorded several of his poems. So did e. e. cummings, Edward Davison, Melville Cane, and Padraic Colum. We also borrowed or rented tapes of recordings by Robert Frost, T. S. Eliot, and Dylan Thomas, who is guaranteed to make even the strongest ramrod of a backbone shiver.

The production team was small but talented: Jerry Newman, the sound engineer, fast, tough, and sensitive to the smallest whisper of a defect in the recording. When it came time to record, we resorted to Jerry's attic on East 26th Street, with its weird hangings and other acoustical shields. It was a strange, casual spot with the finest technical equipment. There was just enough natural friction and rivalry between Arthur Klein and Jerry Newman to keep them both on their toes and bring out their best.

Arthur Klein, with occasional supplementing from me and my friend, Louis Untermeyer, had wide contacts among the good voices and skillful readers of stage and screen, radio, and TV, both in New York and among visiting English actors. I learned that actors rarely are fully occcupied or booked, even many of the big names, and so were, to my delighted surprise, available for recordings such as the *Many Voices* at modest enough fees and/or royalties.

We recruited an admirable cast of twenty-three performers. Most of them came from the stage:

> ALEXANDER SCOURBY, a marvelous voice, by way of Louis Unter-meyer. He gave us a fantastic performance of Poe's "The Bells."
> CYRIL RITCHARD, the immortal "Captain Hook" from *Peter Pan*, who could imprint his natural gaiety on a record.
> MARY MARTIN, *Peter Pan* herself, *South Pacific*, and so on. For us, she did the almost impossible and brought *Evangeline* to life.
> HIRAM SHERMAN, from Broadway, and perhaps the most versatile of all. His reading of Stephen Vincent Benet's "The Mountain Whip-poorwill" is, for me, tops in poetry reading.
> ARNOLD MOSS, successful performer on Broadway, radio, and TV.
> REX INGRAM, fine Negro actor, famous as "De Lawd" in *Green Pastures*.

And from England:

> PAUL ROGERS, star of the Old Vic, and the greatest Macbeth in my theater-going,
> ROSALIND BOXALL, also of the Old Vic and Paul Rogers' wife
> KATHERINE HYNES, of the Old Vic
> E. MARTIN BROWNE, Britain's foremost director of religious drama, and possessor of a beautiful and flexible voice. A saintly man.
> MARTYN GREEN, marvelous Mikado of the D'Oyly Carte Light Opera, before the tragic loss of his leg in an elevator accident

Then came The Great:

> WINSTON CHURCHILL on tape

and descendants of The Great:

RICHARD WORDSWORTH, the great-great-great grandson of the English poet William Wordsworth, with the Old Vic

EDMUND JENNINGS LEE, grandson of General Robert E. Lee, and a clergyman in West Virginia, who read for us Lee's "Farewell to the Army of Virginia"

GEORGE OWEN, a New York Central locomotive engineer, who was born in Ayrshire, Scotland, Robert Burns' home town, and the possessor of a true west-of-Scotland accent. (I got him through the New York Robert Burns Society.)

From literature came:

J. B. PRIESTLEY, playwright and novelist, and a performer on radio and recordings of most entertaining quality

JOHN MASON BROWN, drama critic and columnist for the *Saturday Review*

CLEANTH BROOKS, literary critic, gentle Southern voice, writer of famous textbooks, and professor of English at Yale

From the schools came:

VIRGINIA CHILVER, who directed the choral reading of James Whitcomb Riley's old thing, "Little Orphan Annie." She brought her whole seventh-grade class into Jerry Newman's attic studio to make the recording. The kids had a grand time!

KENT HIEATT from Columbia, Chaucer scholar, to give us authentic thirteenth century accent

I had a long, tough, but finally successful correspondence with Winston Churchill and his secretary to get permission to use a portion of the tape of the great man himself reading his speech "This is their finest hour." I reproduce the key items of the correspondence in Appendix A.

There was other hard bargaining in the drive to get permissions and tapes, notably with the two tough ex-Vassar girls who founded and run Caedmon Records. We had of course to have Dylan Thomas, the greatest of all twentieth century voices, and surely one of the top modern British poets. The pound of flesh that the Caedmon girls exacted for the use of the Dylan Thomas tape of his wonderful poem "Do Not Go Gentle Into That Good Night" was a promise to use my best offices to persuade Carl Sandburg to make an album with Caedmon. I did, Carl consented, and the girls got their album. By contrast, Harvard Vocarium came through, without undue pressure, with the tape of T. S. Eliot reading "The Hollow Men," another memorable recording. And Benjamin Britten was handsome in granting us permission to use his musical setting for Tennyson's "The Bugle Song" from his *Serenade for Tenor, Horn, and Strings,* a fresh and lovely variation among our readings.

Our "record cabinet" decided to use a narrator or commentator on each record to tie the readings together into coherent units and to give hints for fullest appreciation of the readings. I have often wondered why the big record companies so rarely use the device of a commentator on recordings especially suitable for it. Most listeners, and certainly those in classrooms, like to be oriented about what is being read and who is doing it. Sometimes, too, a short preliminary remark can illuminate a whole passage. Besides, using narrators gave me the excuse to add still more glamor to the Olympic *Adventures.*

It was J. B. Priestley who set the pattern for the narrator. He came into the office at 383 Madison Avenue, we talked for ten or fifteen minutes, and then JB said, "Lead me to a typewriter." We did and in about an hour he came up with the first narrator's script, from the great wealth of his experience on BBC during World War Two and his flexible, fluent writing skill. After that some of our narrators wrote their own stuff and were edited, while for others we inside editors wrote the script for them. A good textbook editor, I have always defined, is one who can and does anything in the production of a textbook and its satellites that he can't get anyone else to do.

After twelve or fifteen months of good hard work, we got the *Many Voices* ready to display in pride at the big sales meeting at the Lake Shore Club in Chicago in September, 1957—again in plenty of time for the Texas, Florida, and other important adoptions. These records, most of the salesmen agreed, gave the Olympic *Adventures* a decisive edge over Scott Foresman, Ginn, Singer, and the rest of the literature competition. At any rate the Olympics piled up the best sales record ever, a Himalaya of textbook publishing!

It was in April, 1958 that I started my last big pioneering venture. HB and I had our first encounter with Programmed Instruction (PI for short) in the behavioral laboratories of Dr. B. F. Skinner at Harvard.

wj had first gotten wind of Skinner and pi and soon drew both John McCallum and me into the exploration. In several visits to Skinner's basement on the Harvard campus, his experimental pigeons and rats always quietly noisy nearby, we were all impressed by Dr. Skinner, a truly original inventive genius. I had earlier run across him in the late forties at the University of Indiana but didn't have the wit to latch onto him then. A bit later he invented the famed—or ill-famed, if you are maternal and illogical—"baby box" and he wrote his Utopia, a fascinating book called *Walden Two*. Now in '58 all three of us from HB were impressed, not only by Skinner the man, but also by his first generation teaching machines and the vast rosy promise of pi.

wj had sufficient interest and confidence in pi that he persuaded the Board of Directors to allot $50,000 to develop a teaching machine and the programs to go into it. Soon he arranged a collaboration with Dr. Skinner. He appointed John McCallum to work with Skinner to develop the machine and me to develop programs and have them ready for the machine when it was ready.

I went to Joseph Blumenthal, one of our two star grammar authors and suggested that he work with us to transform his tried, tested, and successful body of teaching materials for high school grammar into a programmed form that could be used in Skinner's teaching machine. Joe's grammar approach was in textbook form (*Living Language*) and in workbook form (*English Work Shops*). Ninth grade, the end of junior high school or the beginning of the four-year high school, seemed the right level for our experiment. Joe turned out to be a natural programmer and he was soon an all-out enthusiast for the programming technique. He worked with Professor Donald E. P. Smith (the initials standing for his subject at the University of Michigan, Educational Psychology), and me all summer and early fall. On schedule, we had the MS for our English grammar program, eventually called *English 2600* (for the number of steps or tiny units it was broken into) all ready to be put on paper tape. But Dr. Skinner and John McCallum had not fared so well with the machine; by early '59 it was agreed by mutual consent that HB had little to contribute to the machine and it was better for Dr. Skinner and HB to part and go our separate ways. We at HB were by then convinced that programmed books rather than teaching machine programs were better for us and for the schools and colleges.

The MS for *English 2600* lay around the shop for a few months in the backwash of the decision not to put it onto paper tape for use in a teaching machine. Then came the idea to make a new kind of workbook, a programmed book. A brilliant design was devised by Stanley Rice, of our Production Department, who himself soon became a topnotch programmer. The MS was revised, tried out in a small way by Blumenthal on a few of his pupils in Detroit, and sent to the printer in the fall of '59. It then took a full year to solve all the new and difficult problems of setting a programmed book in type and printing it, as compared with four to six months to put a conventional book of similar length through the works.

English 2600 came out in October and became an immediate success. It had the full and enthusiastic support of the salesmen and by 1968 it was in its third edition, with sales approaching a million copies. The immediate success of *English 2600* led to our staging a full-dress programming conference, attended by prominent programmers and famous educators. Out of this conference and the rolling sales of the Blumenthal program came WJ's decision to set up our Division of Programmed Instruction in the High School Department with an annual budget of $100,000 and me as the excited, deeply challenged director.

"If I were taking on your new job," said Wil Schramm, my great *Adventures* author and himself caught up in the programming frenzy, as we drove away from the programming conference, "the first thing I'd do would be to write a program myself." I knew he was right, but the prospect scared me. Sure, I had edited some five hundred textbooks over the past three and a half decades and had done a fair amount of incidental writing, but programming was new, different, formidable.

Teaching machines were making a great uproar; they were the new educational panacea. Teachers, school administrators, and publishers were all excited about PI. Wall Street, with understandable delusions over the grandeur of school budgets, and the general public, always open to a new gadget, became aroused. Extremists saw in PI a solution to the continuing shortage of teachers and the need to modernize the school curriculum quickly; they made extravagant claims: "PI is the greatest advance since the printed book." New little companies sprang up and great established companies ranging from U.S. Industries and Kodak to the encyclopedia and textbook firms took the plunge into PI. Funds from the US Office of Education in Washington and Ford and Carnegie Foundations became available to eager researchers. The Center for Programmed Instruction was set up in New York City, headed by a bright mathematics teacher from a New York City private school, Kenneth Komoski, and was steadily supported. There were workshops and conferences all over the country, and the PI movement took on the excited, even frantic aspects of a crusade.

Following the statement by Wil Schramm, I knew I had to try my hand at writing a poetry program. Why poetry? Perhaps because everyone said it was hardest, even impossible. PI is good, the consensus was, in factual subjects where there are precise answers, but don't get into the bog of literature or history, where interpretations vary and everyone knows what he likes. And so it turned out. Programming poetry clearly became the hardest assignment in all my years of text-book editing. But pioneering, though never easy, is always the most satisfying and the most rewarding.

A programmer needs to have or to acquire a doctrine or set of teaching ideas, a body of content to put into programmed form for better teaching and learning. By great good fortune I came upon my "doctrine" in poetry. It was an article by the poet and critic, John Ciardi, "Robert Frost, The Way to the Poem" in the *Saturday Review* which we were anthologizing for one of the Warriner books. In coming on this piece I felt like a small scale Moses seeing the promised land or a tiny Columbus glimpsing a new world. Here were the essential ideas for an eager programmer.

For the next month I took days at home in Connecticut and part of a May vacation to sweat out a draft of this poetry program—altogether about a hundred hours of hard work. I had my wife and daughter as my first guinea pigs to try out the frames or steps of the program on; I had good colleagues in our swiftly growing Department of Programmed Instruction to edit the MS and make me re-write, and teacher-authors like Wil Schramm to criticize and comment; and soon I had John Ciardi himself and Dr. Laurence Perrine, one of our great college authors and a teacher at Southern Methodist University, as collaborators.

During a week of my vacation in middle May I spent an hour on each of five days after school with six juniors and seniors of the Ridgefield High School. They were volunteer "guinea pigs" trying out the poetry program. In addition, the superintendent of schools and the principal of the high school worked the program.

Programming poetry fitted in with the main trend in literature teaching of the fifties and sixties; namely, teach masterpieces, with full attention brought to bear on the work of literature itself, rather than on literary history, social backgrounds, or biographical information; read complete works, rather than selections or abridgements; and engage in intensive examination of the underlying esthetic structure, rather than extensive and surface reading for "enjoyment" and "appreciation," though these latter outcomes are not excluded. Although intensive reading has its roots in the critical writings of Coleridge, and even in the works of earlier critics, this general approach to literature came into prominence in the early 1920's and since that time has often been labeled the "new criticism."

By the fifties the emphasis on the close reading of single works had come to dominate the study of literature in the colleges. Close or intensive reading has several sources. The new criticism was one, and here I. A. Richards, of Cambridge and later of Harvard, was perhaps the most influential theorist. At the University of Chicago, head of the English Department Ronald S. Crane, literary critic Elder Olsen, and my old college roommate Norman F. Maclean, referring to their approach as "neo-Aristotelian," disagreed with some of the general theories of the new critics, but like them, they consistently emphasized the close reading of specific works. But the pivot, the work that was primarily responsible for bringing close reading into the college classroom, was Cleanth Brooks' and Robert Penn Warren's famous *Understanding Poetry* (1939).

Now I suggest that you, the reader, go through a sample program which you will find in Appendix B, page 175.

For about six years the programming effort at HB went on and then it tapered off. Writing, editing and printing a programmed book is more expensive in both time and dollars than publishing a conventional textbook. There is, however, a residue from our programming effort: the Blumenthal programs, now a series of three, continues with some vigor; a Programmed Guide to accompany Hilgard's *Introduction to Psychology* has done much to push the Hilgard sales to the very top in psychology; and others of the sixteen programmed books we sweated out and published continue more or less modestly. In the textbook industry most companies have abandoned their programming effort and the ambitious industrial giants have "walked away" from programming. Ken Komoski's Center for Programmed Instruction has dissolved. The most active programming takes place in training guides for corporations, banks, and trade associations, though some programmed books are creeping back onto textbook publishers lists. And PI has had a definite influence on computerized education. My own book, *Poetry: A Closer Look*, with Ciardi and Perrine, still sells modestly. My son, Jamie, has developed his own small programming company and makes a good living from it. Though teaching machines and PI have so far fallen far short of the original rosy hopes, instructional materials—and the writers and editors of instructional materials—will never be the same again.

The *Adventures* series grew a vigorous new branch beginning in the late fifties: the *Adventures in Good Books* series. It originated, surprisingly, as a response to the growing threat of paperbacks cutting into sales of hardback textbooks in the schools. Paperback books were increasingly used in the schools, mainly because the students like them. They are light, easy to carry, fit into the pocket, can be had for the kind of pocket money high school students have, and they offer a welcome variety. WJ and our salesmen, however, were solidly against our publishing paperback textbooks, though I was strongly tempted. The compromise we worked out was *Adventures in Good Books*, a series eventually consisting of fifteen solid titles. Each book is durably bound in cloth, containing usually four complete books, and yet on a selection basis compares favorably in price with paperbounds. For example, the trailblazer *Four American Novels*, still the best seller in the series, contains:

The Scarlet Letter, by Nathaniel Hawthorne
Moby Dick, by Herman Melville
The Red Badge of Courage, by Stephen Crane
The Bridge of San Luis Rey, by Thornton Wilder

all complete except for a slight abridgement of *Moby Dick*. (The long, dated, and dull whaling history and congeries of facts about whaling were little missed and certainly these excisions may be said to have strengthened rather than weakened the literary quality of the work.)

Most paperbacks were at the time (the late fifties) defective teaching instruments. They lacked study aids such as introductions, study questions, footnotes to explain hard words, dated or recondite terms, afterwords, and teacher's manuals. After a big conference of executives, editors, and salesmen, I set out in the usual hurry to build the series. I telephoned Edmund Fuller, that rare creature: an active practicing classroom teacher who is also a creative writer of national standing. Edmund was teaching at the Kent School in Connecticut and he had a fine reputation as novelist and literary critic. He was ambitious, welcomed a chance to make some surefire royalties, and saw the challenge of our war on the paperbacks. Right away he said, "Yes." Soon we recruited other leading literary lights:

LEON EDEL, the great authority on biography
CLIFTON FADIMAN, versatile literateur
JOHN T. FREDERICK, the short-story writer and novelist
FRANK G. JENNINGS, editor-at-large of the *Saturday Review*
WALTER KERR, drama critic of the New York *Herald Tribune*
J. B. PRIESTLEY, the fabulous versatile writer from England

and teamed them up with star teachers from the public and private schools.

One innovation in the editorial approach is noteworthy. We shifted from the usual long introduction, which was pretty meaningless until the student had read the selection itself, to a short, interest-arousing introduction or teaser and then really shot the works on an afterword. Here our writer held a "conversation" with the student-reader. It was much better than the conventional apparatus. *Adventures in Good Books* books were all single column, easy to read—and inexpensive. They did, and are still, doing well.

A delightful extra dividend was the association with Edmund Fuller, now a literary critic and book reviewer for the *Wall Street Journal*. Edmund has one of the most glorious beards of our times, a fine-flowing slightly curly beard, unstreaked by grey, and when he came striding out of the water at Great Pond where we were wont to swim, he looked like the old seagod Neptune himself. Edmund could write to prescription and turn out a fine literary piece on any topic. His taste and judgment were good, and when combined with my original and often bizarre suggestions, we made a series that had longlast quality.

Early in 1958 wj asked me to take some time to do some traveling and investigate whether hb should enter the field of elementary reading, and if so, how. Over a period of about four months I traveled twelve thousand miles, interviewed one hundred twenty-five people from coast to coast, keeping a diary as was my custom on ms and other trips, and finally was ready to draw up my report. Two secretaries came out to our home in Ridgefield, Connecticut, sat on the lawn with me, and over two days I dictated my report of some twenty thousand words. I wound it up with the recommendation that we enter elementary publishing by working with the great English philosopher, linguist, and poet, I. A. Richards, now set up in his own messy little shop at Harvard, with his associate, Christine Gibson. wj and I figured we would follow through by working with Paul Brandwein, who was all ripe for it, on an elementary science series.

All this was most plausible, but the Board of Directors was not buying it. At this stage the Board was pretty imagination-bound. They tended to be worried by the rapid growth of our textbook business and the consequent large expansion of the Company's need to borrow from the banks in the spring and summer months. The banks weren't worried but some of the directors were. Relations were further strained by wj's wanting a contract for himself, which the Board was reluctant to give and finally never did offer to him. So the directors turned down our plans for expanding into elementary publishing.

wj, John McCallum, and I were pretty upset about this rejection and for a time considered jumping the reservation and going to another company. I arranged quiet talks between Armand Erpf, my old friend at Loeb, Rhoades and now chairman of the Finance Committee at Crowell Collier, and John McCallum. But Armand, rather to our surprise, did not jump at the opportunity to acquire what we modestly— but accurately, I still insist—thought to be the hottest team in all textbook publishing. Negotiations faded away. Still unhappy, I approached, with WJ's knowledge and consent, Curtis Benjamin of McGraw-Hill about my going over there (with Paul Brandwein, who said he would go where I'd go) but Benjamin too said, "No." Actually I think we were all glad no final rupture had taken place. The better way to get into elementary publishing, rather than to start from scratch, was to pick up an already existing elementary company and build with it. This was the advice of my old Dartmouth friend and Toledo industrialist, Edward Lamb, and it is what WJ and JHM did in fact do when HB acquired the World Book Company in 1960.

Along in 1960 the urge to expand by acquisition became overpowering for us. First we looked at Silver Burdett, one of the good elementary publishers, headed by Burr Chase, and my old friend and fraternity mate, Charles Griffith, talented violinist and prime developer of Silver's superb music department. George White had worked for Silver for many years before they moved to New Jersey and George came to us. But somehow the dialogue didn't ripen properly at the time and eventually Silver sold themselves to Time, Inc.—which in my opinion has badly mishandled this fine textbook company.

WJ and JHM did get in touch with the World Book Company, of Tarrytown, New York. The time was ripe, WJ and William Ferguson, their president, had a mutually satisfactory dialogue, and HB bought World, to become Harcourt, Brace & World. A little before the consummation of these corporate nuptials, HB "went public," that is, its stock was hypothecated by White, Weld and Company, one of the very bright Wall Street brokers, and launched us into orbit on August 17, 1960.

CHAPTER NINE

ORGANIZING THE TALENT
AN OVERVIEW

Whatever you can do, or dream you can, begin it.
Boldness has genius, power, and magic in it.
                                    Goethe

LOOKING BACK AT MY SENIOR YEAR PAPER at Dartmouth, "Freethinking Pragmatism," some forty years later, I feel no sense of shame. My feelings are mixed, but most of them are on the positive side. Its main positions I still hold.

Today, in this century's sixties—and mine too—I have even less need for the mediation of religious ideas between the inner core of myself and outer reality. I have raised three children of my own and had a parental relationship with at least two other young ones, without leaning on Christianity or other religions. God seems even less relevant today than He did in 1924.

The resolution in my senior paper of the old free will vs. determinism conflict has served me well in the publishing experience. I still believe that men do have choices and that an individual decision can influence outcomes; or, as I put it then, "a man with his brain can be and often is one link in a sequence of effective causes and so can exert some control over results." This activist attitude of mine early hooked up with a similar attitude of AH's. He often said in making a close editorial decision about whether to go ahead with a project or to reject or get out of it, "If you throw your full energies into the struggle—and stick with it—you can make a success of this project. Go ahead!"

I still would say, as I did forty-odd years ago, that the truth is that which works, and it's a matter of choosing the set of "fictions" that is most convenient. But choosing among alternative "sets of fictions" is not so easy or simple as I then thought. By what criteria or scale of values does one make the choice and cast the die? For one thing, I have developed a "scale of people": at the apex are the poets (Sandburg, Frost, Untermeyer, Ciardi) and research scientists (George Gaylord Simpson, Ernest R. Hilgard). They are the finest, most interesting, and oddly enough the longest-lived! Just a shade below my apex are the good writers (J. B. Priestley, Wil Schramm, many others). Then come the good teachers, scores of them. Editors and salesmen and executives are all right but, with me, they don't have the wispy touch of idealism my top three categories have. Thus, it was no accident that a good many poets, major and minor, became involved, over the years in the *Adventures* series. Or that two of the great books of the College Department came from the research scientists.

My firm base in psychology is still firm and I hold to the modern psychologists' view of human nature and I have confidence in the healing skills of psychiatrists.

The aesthetic views expressed in "Free-thinking Pragmatism" today impress me as being pretty heavily eroded by time and change; they have faded with the proper and appropriate fading of my youthful romanticism. But on the whole this paper of my senior year was not only fun to write at one big swoop but fun to live out—over the years.

The editor of textbooks has a number of advantages over the editor of trade books. For one thing, there is less guesswork; there are many more knowns in the textbook equation. In publishing books for sale to the public through bookstores, book clubs and the like, there is much folklore but few, if any, reliable formulas. Textbooks in both college and high school must fit courses; and the larger the fraction of the text material for a course that one textbook can supply the better its chances for large and long use in the course it fits. The courses are large in number and great in their variety, but both number and variety are finite; they can be known and their requirements met by a hard-working textbook editor and a supporting cast of salesmen. In contrast, the editor of trade books has access to fewer salesmen and is more likely to have a "teacher-student" relationship to them than the more normal "co-worker" relationship in the textbook department. The wise textbook editor does a good bit of traveling on his MS trips to the colleges, or on trips with the high school salesmen to assist in big adoptions or simply to travel in a salesman's territory and get to know him and it better. The rear end of the trade editor is more apt to stay planted in the editorial chair and to leave it mainly for conferences within the shop or for long lunches over the driest of martinis with authors or agents. Literary agents, thank heavens, still rarely infest the world of textbooks.

Of course for sheer glamor the textbook editor must bow to the trade editor. Maxwell Perkins, Scribner's great trade editor, worked with Ernest Hemingway, Thomas Wolfe, and F. Scott Fitzgerald; Alfred Harcourt with Carl Sandburg, Sinclair Lewis, and Dorothy Canfield. Sometimes too, the trade editor has a discernible impact on the final product. It is reputed, for example, that it was Maxwell Perkins who cut Wolfe's MSS down to size and gave them their final shape. And legendary Saxe Cummins at Random House worked wonders with William Faulkner's sometimes impenetrable MSS. But, perhaps more often, the trade editor is mainly a drinking companion, a sympathetic ear, and in the great author's declining years a wet nurse. Alfred Harcourt in 1930 did not fight to hold Sinclair Lewis on the HB list when from Copenhagen after receiving his Nobel Prize in Stockholm Lewis cabled for his release. But the personal ties that bind trade author and trade editor are often powerful: T. S. Eliot and Thomas Merton and Robert Lowell left HB with Robert Giroux in 1954 when he joined Farrar & Straus.

The impact of a textbook editor on the final book can be, and often is, large and impressive. The trade author generally wants little or no editing; he has shaped a work of art and that's that. The college author is usually a master of his subject matter; none of us in College Editorial could add a jot or tittle of biology to G. G. Simpson's MS for *Life*. What a good and sensible inside college editor can do is to apply "the amateur test": if he (the editor) can't understand something, then he is entitled to question it, get the author to fix it, or re-write it himself. High school authors, even the good ones, generally need more guidance from the editor. Unlike many of the competitors—and some of my successors at HB—I have always greatly valued the author. The great danger in having textbooks composed inside the publisher's shop is that the books are homogenized. A healthy and stimulating tension between author and editor has disappeared and with it some of the author's quirks, cranks, and idiosyncrasies that make for color and interest. Instead, there's a tendency toward a neutral grey—safe enough but generally dull. House-written textbooks have the sharpness of a fifth carbon copy!

The good textbook editor is alert and sensitive to trends in his special subjects. Always I tried to be one, or one and a half, not two jumps ahead of the great moderate mass of teachers. I wanted to be a pioneer and innovator, not a follower or imitator, as some publishers are—by design. One prominent textbook president actually said to me, "We wait until you or some one else has found and established a good new thing and then we come in and do it better or cheaper." But mostly he's wrong: the inventor can usually do it better than any imitator or late-comer. Provided he doesn't sit back and relax.

Always I tried, first, to make visible superior features and, second, to be swift to revise before we began to slip or the competitors to make serious inroads. It was wise, I found, not to rely on just one good new feature but rather to pile on several. This one-two punch, revisions plenty soon and multiple strong features, enabled us greatly to extend the active life of our big books and series.

The tradition once was that a textbook, even with revisions, could expect at most a good active life of about ten or twelve years, like Hitchcock for Holt and Ward for Scott Foresman in the teens and twenties. Chapman's *Using English* lasted just about its expected span. But the *Adventures* series was second to *Literature and Life* for its first fifteen years (1927-1942), then became first in the field in 1942, and began to split into so many tributary series by 1968 that it was difficult to make any sort of claim whatsoever—like a great river splitting up over its delta and finally disappearing out to sea. *Exploring Biology*, Casner & Gabriel, the Warriners, *The College Omnibus*, Hilgard, Hodges, Simpson—all have had the stamina for lengthy royalty-bearing lives.

Sometimes, an outsider on Wall or some other street will ask about "Research and Development" in the Textbook Industry. There is mighty little, as such. Our good authors are the researchers and developers, like Joe Blumenthal and his "small specialty, twenty years of teaching grammar to high school pupils" or John Hodges and his file of freshman themes, kept, studied, and analyzed over three and a half decades.

Finally, in sheer volume of sales the trade editor can rarely compete with the textbook editor. The *Adventures* series, to take my most potent example, has over the years reached well over 100 million students. Furthermore, each copy sold has been used not only by about five students, but each student has spent a good part of a school year in reading and studying his *Adventures* volume. It is not just entertainment for a few pleasant or exciting hours as with the good trade book. One form of contemporary literary immortality for an author is to be published in the *Adventures* series. Some authors— Dorothy Canfield, Paul deKruif, even e. e. cummings—were mindful of this and always most cooperative. And Bernard Shaw and Thornton Wilder, as well as HB, have benefited from the inclusion of *Pygmalion* and *Our Town* in the *Adventures* series.

The impact of a good-sized textbook operation, the president of the University of Illinois once told AH, is about as big as that of a good-sized university. I don't know how to measure a thing like that, but we did much to

- bring twentieth century literature into the school curriculum
- reduce the cost of textbooks in the Depression
- induce poets and other good creative people to participate in the building of textbooks
- introduce cartoons and color and folksongs and other unexpected things into high school books
- join safety to health and so help to maintain both
- apply the "omnibus" idea to college freshman English and to French
- reduce excessive science terminology in textbooks
- do some pioneering in literature recordings and film strips
- publish on the educationally progressive side, not merely the nakedly profitable side
- appeal to the best, the most intelligent teachers and schools
- teach big understandings, not facts for their own sakes
- back the integrity of good authors against various opportunisms
- give a new direction, occasionally, to a subject

— introduce the technique of the symposium to college textbook
publishing

— keep a constant flow of fresh editorial and author talent into the
textbooks

— keep on the alert to take full advantage of new technical developments in book manufacture

— anticipate and meet the changing needs of the schools and colleges

— protect the author from undue pressure from the sales force

The good editor-in-chief of textbooks has to have the knack of recruiting not only good authors (that goes without saying), but also
from the sales force or the schools good inside editors, copyeditors,
and secretaries. I rarely hired people from competitors or from job
agencies. The most important are the inside editors, for it is they who
do the final close editing of the MSS, supervise the copyediting, the art
work, coordinate the work of the whole team, and shepherd the MS
and its satellites through the works—*on schedule* in order to quiet the
howls of the salesmen. My best short definition of the job of the textbook editor still is that he does himself what he can't get anyone else
to do, a requirement exacting the utmost versatility.

After recruiting, logically comes training and here is where I myself
think I have done the poorest job, although some of the good editors
who worked with me say otherwise. Perhaps the key expression here
is "work with," for I have never thought of myself primarily as a
"boss." How can one "train" a Jovanovich, or a McCallum, or a Deighton? The best thing one can do is to unleash them.

The editor-in-chief can generate and maintain an atmosphere which
encourages free interchange. I kept my door constantly open and urged
my editors to stick their heads in and always to feel free to bring their
problems in. Mainly, the editor-in-chief educates or trains by an example of concentration and hard work, and by tackling the hardest
jobs himself.

Fairly early I instituted the policy of HB paying the tuition of any
editor or copyeditor who wished to improve himself by taking courses
in editing or publishing at Columbia or NYU. A number of my people did avail themselves of the sometimes excellent courses offered

there. Occasionally I made an appearance and gave a lecture or two at Saxe Cummins' course in book publishing in the School of General Studies at Columbia.

In 1959, when my editorial force in the High School Department was reaching what then seemed the astronomical total of sixty people, I organized "Editorial 22," a course of 22 weekly sessions, each an hour in length, to present a survey of the total editorial process—from gleam in the eye to finished book. Attendance was compulsory and we would gather in the big Directors Room at 750 Third Avenue, to which the Company had emigrated in 1958. I gave most of the talks and introduced others to give theirs: Kermit Patton on production, Stanley Rice on book design, Mike Miller on book design, Don Stewart on social studies, Dorothy Snowman on copyediting, Don Meyer and Paul Brandwein on science, Newbury Morse on foreign language, and so on. Was "Editorial 22" a success? I really couldn't tell, for the demand for a repeat was not overwhelming.

Of equal importance with training is the nerve to give responsibility, the real developer, to good people, when they are ripe—or almost ripe —for it. Promotions can help. As the editorial staff grew in size, I developed a small hierarchy or ranking system: assistant editor, associate editor, editor. I also organized High School Editorial by subjects and put one of my best in charge of each: social studies under Don Stewart, French under Newbury Morse, science under Don Meyer, copyediting under Grace Carlson and later Dorothy Snowman. I did not delegate power over my truelove, English literature and composition, though Jim Russell soon developed as right bower.

Then there is the seamy side of the job of the editor-in-chief: he has to fire, as well as hire. I don't know any other way of building a really strong editorial staff than by careful, intuitive hiring and strong-minded fact-facing when and if it comes time to do some firing.

Well-timed pay-raising is of course another useful tool. Oddly enough, I myself never asked for a salary increase or negotiated an increase in my own compensation all those years at HB. Partly it was pride: I wouldn't petition. Partly it was naïveté, but mostly it was confidence in myself and my future and in the fairness of the highest echelon.

After HB went public in 1960 and merged with World Book Company to become Harcourt, Brace & World, it was never the same again. The Company suffered a sea change. I stayed on for three years, worked hard at building and helping the mighty expansion, and finally WJ suggested that I retire. I did not argue. John McCallum decided to pull out a few months later and WJ was "king of the hill." He and HBW went on to bigger and bigger things. Thus ended my great—and mostly happy—adventure in textbooks.

It *has* been an adventure. There have been heavy costs along with fine rewards. I am mindful now only of the joint efforts, the joy of achievement, the celebrations. Out of these have developed special relationships and enduring friendships, which I cherish. We may find ourselves slipping off into different rooms, but the building is ours.

APPENDIX A

THE CHURCHILL CORRESPONDENCE

January 10, 1957

Sir Winston Churchill
Chartwell House
Westaham
Kent, England

Sir:

We are most desirous of including your recording of the enclosed selection from your great World War II speech "This was their finest hour" in Many Voices 6B, one of the two long play records we are making to accompany our 12th grade anthology *Adventures In English Literature*, Olympic edition.

Just before Christmas we applied to Columbia Records for permission to re-record this small part of their 12 inch long play record "I Can Hear It Now" volume 4. Their reply was as follows:

"As you will note from the restriction notice contained on our album cover, the material contained in the speeches embodied on the record is owned by Sir Winston Churchill. The permission granted to us to use this material, which was obtained after a substantial payment by us to Sir Winston, was specifically restricted to the use of the material on records distributed by our company and consisting of material previously approved by Sir Winston."

For your background I am enclosing a tentative list of selections from *Adventures in English Literature* that we plan to record on the two records to accompany *Adventures in English Literature*. We strongly feel that these records would be lamentably inadequate without the voice of Winston Churchill. It would be almost like Shakespeare's *Hamlet* without *Hamlet*.

It will perhaps interest you to know that J. B. Priestley is to be the Narrator on both records for this volume and that Paul Rogers of the Old Vic, Richard Wordsworth (great, great grandson of the Poet) and E. Martin Browne of the British Drama League are also contributing. We are reproducing T. S. Eliot's own reading of "The Hollow Men" and Dylan Thomas' "Do Not Go Gentle Into That Good Night."

We can offer you a small royalty—1/2¢ per record sold with an advance of $25.00 against this royalty. Since this is the first time we ever attempted to make records to go with our textbooks, I literally have no idea what sale to expect. My best hunch is that it will be considerably more than necessary to earn the advance.

Won't you consider all this and if, as I hope, you are favorably inclined to insure that each new generation of American high school students will hear the voice of Winston Churchill, please cable me collect.

Very truly yours,

James M. Reid
Editor of the School
Textbook Department

P.S.   So that you may see also the anthology which the records are to accompany, I am sending you by Airmail a copy of *Adventures in English Literature*, Mercury edition. The Olympic edition referred to above is the revision we are publishing in 1958.

Roquebrune, A.M.
28 January, 1957

Dear Mr. Reid,

Sir Winston Churchill has asked me to thank you for your letter of January 10. He is indeed sorry that he cannot accede to your request. He has received many similar suggestions and for a number of reasons has felt obliged to decline them all. I am so sorry.

Yours sincerely,

Private Secretary

Mr. James M. Reid

February 7, 1957

Sir Winston Churchill
Chartwell House
Westaham
Kent, England

Dear Sir:

I have a note from your secretary turning down our request for permission to use the recording of a passage from your famous speech "This was their finest hour," in my letter of January 10. This puts us in a rather silly position which I should like to explain and ask you to reconsider.

As I indicated in my first letter, we are using this passage from your speech in our anthology, *Adventures in English Literature* Olympic edition. We did not ask your permission because it, like all speeches of heads of governments, is in the public domain. Our lawyers tell me that a performer has no legal rights in his performance. The situation seems to be, therefore, that there is no legal reason which could stop us from re-recording your own performance of this passage from your speech. However, there is a moral reason, and I assure you that we would not re-record your performance of this speech without your express permission.

We feel that Many Voices 6A and 6B, the recordings we are preparing to accompany *Adventures in English Literature:* Olympic edition absolutely have to have a reading of your speech. We would be open to serious criticism from the thousands of teachers in American high schools who are giving the course in English literature. The refusal in your secretary's letter of January 28 thus forces us to make other arrangements. At the present time we are inclined to ask J. B. Priestley to record the speech for us, or if he cannot then we could find here in New York a skilled actor to do it. But this is so second best that I make bold to ask you to reconsider your decision.

I understand that you have never particularly been interested in royalty arrangements. May I suggest then that we double the advance suggested in my letter of January 10, and offer you a flat fee of $50 for your permission to re-record the part of the speech we requested in that letter. Since we need to move fast, may I respectfully request that you cable me collect your decision.

Respectfully yours,

James M. Reid
Editor of the School
Textbook Department

28 Hyde Park Gate
London, S.W. 7
4 February, 1957

Dear Sirs:

I am desired by Sir Winston Churchill to thank you very much for sending him a copy of *Adventures in English Literature*, which he has received with interest.

Yours truly,

Private Secretary

Messrs. Harcourt, Brace & Co.

Roquebrune-Cap Martin, A.M.
6 March, 1957

Dear Mr. Reid,

I write on behalf of Sir Winston Churchill in reply to your letter of February 7. Under English law, speeches of "heads of government" are not "in public domain," and it would be a breach of the copyright law if any of Sir Winston's speeches were copied. Any public speech after delivery may be reported in the newspapers, but this does not give anyone the right to make any other use of the speech subsequently. Possibly the American position is different.
Sir Winston is ready, however, to allow exceptionally your use of the passage which you enclosed with your letter of January 10.

Yours sincerely,

Private Secretary

Mr. James M. Reid

A SAMPLE OF PROGRAMMED INSTRUCTION

THIS SAMPLE PROGRAM IS the central part of the finished program, Steps 41 through 80, which are intended to guide a close reading of Frost's "Stopping by Woods on a Snowy Evening." The complete program, from Reid, Ciardi, and Perrine's book, *Poetry: A Closer Look*, seeks (1) to improve the attitude of high school students toward poetry and (2) to start them developing for themselves a method which can become a permanent part of their repertoire for reading poems in depth. Programmed Instruction makes no claims to perfection. Good literature is always a various, supple, and multiple engagement between the reader and the author. The good reader learns to read in that multiple way. But the beginning must go step by step. Now, if you will, please read the Frost poem carefully, thoughtfully.

Stopping by Woods on a Snowy Evening
by
Robert Frost

Whose woods these are I think I know.
His house is in the village though.
He will not see me stopping here
To watch his woods fill up with snow.

My little horse must think it queer   5
To stop without a farmhouse near

Between the woods and frozen lake
The darkest evening of the year.

He gives his harness bells a shake
To ask if there is some mistake.   10
The only other sound's the sweep
Of easy wind and downy flake.

The woods are lovely, dark and deep,
But I have promises to keep,
And miles to go before I sleep,   15
And miles to go before I sleep.

The next reading is guided by the program. You cannot read or go through a program as you read a traditional book or magazine or newspaper article. You can't even use the Evelyn Woods speed reading techniques on PI. You need to collaborate with the program, step by step, responding actively as you go. As Edmund Fuller of Kent School says, "A program is a kind of exploded essay, with questions or statements with blanks or choices in them, inviting the active participation of the reader to complete the essay."

People have actively to experience, not just read a program to understand what PI is about. If you "skim" or glance through a program you will be confused and you will dislike it thoroughly.

Please secure a file card or piece of paper to use as a book mark. Place the book mark over the answer in the righthand column and don't look at the response to a step. It is best to write your response to each step on a separate piece of paper; so doing makes for greater involvement. But a mental or implicit response will do. When you have responded to a step, check your answer with the program's answer in the righthand column. Then go on, step by step. Now make your start and feel free to refer to the poem as you go along. Average reading time for this section of the program is 30 minutes.

Exploring The Larger Meanings

(41)
Before digging deeper into the poem, let us understand an important word: *symbol.* You are familiar with many symbols. The fox is a sym-

bol of craftiness. A white flag is a _____ of surrender or truce. A king's crown is a _____ of his authority.

(41)
_____
symbol
symbol

(42)
A symbol, then, brings to mind or stands for "something-else." The incident narrated in "Stopping by Woods" contains a number of _____. It suggests meanings that are far beyond the surface meaning of the narrative.

(42)
_____
symbols

(43)
Let us see if we can discover the symbols in "Stopping by Woods." To do this, we will have to examine each detail in the poem and ask what is the "something-else" it brings to mind or _____ for.

(43)
_____
stands

(44)
By looking at the poem again, you are reminded that the narrator had four things pressing on his mind: (1) his thinking about the owner in the _____; (2) the impatience of the little _____; (3) the attraction of the _____, "dark and deep"; and (4) the "miles to go" and the "_____ to keep."

(44)
_____
village
horse
woods
promises

(45)
Let us examine the first thing that was on his mind. Why is the owner of the woods men-

tioned in the poem? Is he a symbol? If so, is there a "s_____-e_____" the owner stands for?

(45)

_____

something-else

(46)
The force the owner represents is probably the village, with all its social duties and conflicts. At the very least, Frost may be using the owner as the _____ for village life, with its many people as opposed to the loneliness of the woods.

(46)

_____

symbol

(47)
Frost could also intend to have the owner symbolize those who stay in sheltered places. Or, he could mean those who congregate, rather than _____ by themselves.

(47)

_____

stand, stay
(or synonym)

(48)
The village may even represent not only a particular village in New England but the total "v_____" of civilization.

(48)

_____

village

(49)
The narrator, at least for this instant, seems to have separated himself from the village, the symbol for civilization. Here, stopping by the woods, he is alone, separated, cut off from _____.

(49)

_____

civilization, others
(or synonym)

(50)
Another way of stating this idea is to say that the owner is the representative or _____ of a part of life from which the narrator has temporarily separated himself. He, the narrator, is separated from civilization.

(51)
The driver of the sleigh is one man alone facing the natural forces that every man _____ in his life on earth.

(52)
Our first symbol, then, is the owner of the woods, who represents the v_____, social life, and ultimately civilization.

(53)
You will recall the little horse. He shows his impatience by shaking his _____ bells and thus bringing up the question, "Why did the driver stop?"

(54)
The horse has a special function: he is a *foil*. That is, he is a character who "plays against" the main character. The horse acts as an opposing force against the _____.

---

(50)

---

symbol

(51)

---

faces

(52)

---

village

(53)

---

harness

(54)

---

narrator
(or synonym)

(55)
Thus the horse serves to highlight or bring out the more important character. The horse is the foil for the _____, the main character of the poem.

(55)
_____

man, narrator, speaker, driver

(56)
In opposing the main character and thus serving as a f_____, the horse moves the man to examine more deeply his reasons for stopping by the woods.

(56)
_____

foil

(57)
But by now the horse has also come to stand for something-else. He is not merely a foil for the man. As the village is our first symbol, the horse has become our second _____.

(57)
_____

symbol

(58)
The little horse is a symbol of what "something-else"? He represents a kind of life that does not understand why a man should stop by a patch of woods to watch the snow come down. In this respect, a horse differs from a _____.

(58)
_____

man, human being

(59)
In contrast to the world of civilization symbolized by the owner, the little horse _____ the animal or brute world.

(59)
_____

symbolizes, represents, stands for

(60)
Let us turn to a third possible symbol. Perhaps there is a single "something-else" represented by the woods, the cold, the dark, the frozen lake, and the falling snow. By now we begin to sense that all this lovely dark-and-deep has a powerful attraction for the _____.

(60)
_____
man (or synonym)

(61)
The attraction of the dark and the snow and the woods might be interpreted as the attraction of beauty. Beauty is certainly one aspect of the scene and, therefore, one meaning of the symbol, but this explanation (does/does not) exhaust the meaning of the symbol.

(61)
_____
Your answer
(Most readers of poetry would say does not.)

(62)
One interpretation is that the man feels an invitation from these woods to final surrender and rest. A man may be attracted by these intangible, almost unknowable things, but not an animal, such as the little _____.

(62)
_____
horse

(63)
Some readers of this poem go even further and say that the attraction of the woods represents a wish to die, however momentary. Death, to many people, implies rest and release or es____ from responsibility.

(63)
_____
escape

(64)
No matter how attractive an experience may be, a person may wish to be out of it if the experience involves heavy responsibilities. A football star, for example, might wish momentarily that the big game were over, so that he could be _____ from his responsibilities.

(64)
_____

released, freed
(or synonym)

(65)
At the end of stanza three, the narrator gets a last call from the darkness ". . . the sweep/Of easy wind and downy flake." It would seem so e_____y to go into the woods and let himself be covered over.

(65)
_____

easy

(66)
The man now has three worlds or kinds of life exerting conflicting pulls on him: (1) the social world of the owner; (2) the _____ world of the horse; (3) the dark world within himself which is evoked by the all-engulfing snow and the d_____ness outside.

(66)
_____

animal or brute
darkness

(67)
Furthermore, several things in the poem suggest that the man is on some kind of errand or journey. Is the specific purpose of this journey stated anywhere in the poem? _____

(67)
_____

No

(68)

182

We may ask, then, why the poet doesn't make the speaker tell us what _____ he is on. He might have been going to the general store or to visit Old Aunt Harriet or to do any number of things.

(68)

---

errand, business, journey

(69)
In studying poetry, the reader should assume that every detail in the poem is there by the poet's specific act of choice. Frost clearly _____ not to specify the errand. He left it general or unspecified.

(69)

---

chose
(or synonym)

(70)
Frost indicates that the man is going somewhere, but he clearly chose to leave the nature of the journey unspecified or generalized. He may have intended to suggest any _____ in life and, thereby, to leave the meaning on the broadest level—that is, to use the journey as a symbol.

(70)

---

journey
(or synonym)

(71)
Attracted by the woods part way on his journey, the man has passed—perhaps to work out a mental conflict. He has "promises to keep" at the end of his journey. One part of this sensitive, thinking man would like to give up the conflict, that is, to surrender. But another part is aware of social duties or responsibilities. He must now end this mental con_____. He must *decide*.

(71)

---

conflict

(72)

The thought of the "lovely, dark and deep" woods lingers, but the man's final decision is to cast off the mood and continue his _____. He has promises to keep and _____ to go before he sleeps. He repeats that thought, and the performance ends.

(72)

journey
(or synonym)
miles

(73)

But why did Frost repeat the final line, "And miles to go before I sleep"? The surface meaning is: "I have a long way to go before I get to bed tonight." The second time he says it, however, "miles to go" and "sleep" are turned into _____. Let us consider what these "something-elses" may be.

(73)

symbols (If you wrote "something-elses," you had the right idea.)

(74)

Hundreds of people asked Robert Frost the question, "What are those 'something-elses' that the words in the repeated last lines symbolize?" And Frost always turned this question away because he *could not answer it*, at least not all of it. Poets and poems pose questions, but they do not always _____ the questions in full.

(74)

answer or explain

(75)

A symbol is like a rock dropped into a pool. It sends out ripples in all directions, and the _____ themselves are in motion. It is impossible to say where the last ripple disappears.

ripples

(76)
At the end of "Stopping by Woods," the second "miles to go" may mean "the road of life." Perhaps the second "before I sleep" comes close to _____ "before I take my final rest."

(76)

meaning,
symbolizing
(or synonym)

(77)
In poetry, "sleep" is often used as a symbol for death. The symbolic interpretation of Frost's repeated _____ lines may well be: "And years to live before I die."

(77)

last
(or synonym)

(78)
If we accept this interpretation, it suggests a parallel or close connection between contemplation of the beauty of the woods and a certain giving up or even _____.

(78)

dying, death,
surrender

(79)
The contemplation of beauty, the poet seems to be saying, deserves its place in a full life, but not at the expense of one's obligations and duties. To surrender to beauty at the sacrifice of duty is equivalent to one's (death/survival) as a responsible person.

(79)

death

(80)
In "Stopping by Woods," the narrator, after moments of mental conflict, accepts the _____ he has made, though not without regret.

(80)

---

choice
(or decision)

INDEX

INDEX

INDEX